Civil Disobedience and the Christian

Civil Disobedience
● ◄ ◄
and the
Christian

DANIEL B. STEVICK

 THE SEABURY PRESS · NEW YORK

to the students

Preface

: :

This book is an inquiry into the relation between Christian obedience and responsible civil disobedience. Needless to say, the book was conceived and written in response to contemporary events. I began it several years ago at the height of the civil rights campaign, dropped it during several months spent outside the country (I had the naïve feeling on my return that the issue was dead), and resumed it during protests over the Vietnam war. Resistance to civil authority constitutes today something of a test case for many basic attitudes and loyalties. Conflict between what are understood to be the claims of Caesar and the claims of God is bringing to a focus much of the heroism and cowardice, pettiness and dignity, hardness and compassion of our society. Yet I have drawn on this record of terror and sublimity only rather selectively. The whole story ought to be told someday by someone whose purpose is other than mine. My treatment of the theme is, within the limits of a nontechnical book of modest length, general and analytic. I mean only to isolate the issue: "Is it ever right or permissible in conscience to break a law?" and to consider this ethical problem without extended reference to concrete cases. If the resultant treatment lacks the smell of battle, I hope it has compensating advantages in the applicability of some of its thinking to the many and varied contexts in which decisions are being required of conscientious persons today. I do not intend to make a case for or against civil disobedience in any specific modern situation so much as:

to argue that there are some situations in which civil disobedience is an allowable consideration or an actual duty, to plead for understanding and support for those who are convinced that they are in one of those situations now, to provide criteria by which a person might be assisted in determining that he was or was not obliged to engage in a conscientious violation of law, and to suggest considerations which might make such an action more, rather than less, responsible.

The depressing material delivered to those of us on clergy mailing lists and the letters, articles, and editorials in the religious press indicate that there is widespread categorical rejection of civil disobedience in the Christian community—as well as a great deal of concern and confusion. In the past few years, some official church bodies have made statements on civil disobedience for the guidance of Christian persons. These statements are usually brief and well worded. But in themselves they are inadequate to articulate a Christian stance on a matter which sharply divides most churches. Understanding can only be hoped for from a fuller exposition of the argument behind the statements. The official pronouncements that are worth heeding have the force and consistency they do because they grow out of a context of Christian theological and ethical thought. Terse statements may not be comprehensible to readers with little previous acquaintance with that context. Few statements, however official, can carry much external authority. They must compel assent by the cogency of the ideas they set forth. Some fuller argumentation would seem to be desirable if new ideas are to be weighed on their merits and if unfamiliar duties are to be accepted as truly binding.

The range of material pertinent to the subject of this book proved quite surprising. I am indebted to a number of persons without whose help the treatment would not have even such adequacy as it has. My colleague, Dr. W. Hayden McCallum, read each portion of the manuscript as it was drafted, and there is no chapter which has not been improved by his always helpful criticisms. His generosity with his time and interest has contributed greatly to this book—though, of course, he is not to be implicated in its defects. I was encouraged to pick up again the abandoned notes on civil disobedience by the efforts of several students to formulate a stance in the matter and through an observation of my dean, the Very Reverend Edward G. Harris, that an informed study of the subject did not seem to exist. The notes to Chapter Two indicate the point at which my organization of the New Testament material is indebted to the orderly mind of Dr. John Reumann of the Lutheran Theological Seminary of Philadelphia. Some of the church statements cited in Appendix II had been gathered by the office of Dr. J. Edwin Espy in preparation for the drafting of the statement on civil disobedience by the General Board of the National Council of Churches. I was fortunate to be able to draw on this work. Earlier forms of portions of the material of this book were presented to various church and community groups in the Philadelphia area (the Philadelphia Clericus and the Metropolitan Associates of Philadelphia deserve special mention) as well as to several classes and to the Alumni Association of the Philadelphia Divinity School. Comments and questions at each of these presentations aided in the further development of the manuscript. Perhaps a word of gratitude should be added to all of those persons whose oral comments or writings have indicated to me their fundamental disagreement with the thesis of this book. Without the necessity of reckoning with their ideas, this book would have been easier to write, but it would have been far less adequately argued.

Contents

: :

one
: :
WHAT THE ISSUE IS
AND IS NOT

Martin Luther King, Jr., in his account of the civil rights
campaign at Birmingham, Alabama, speaks of a court injunction obtained by the city administration on April 10, 1963,
directing that demonstrations be halted until the right to such
activities might be argued in court. Dr. King continues: "Two
days later, we did an audacious thing, something we had never
done in any other crusade. We disobeyed a court order." The
importance of the decision was understood at the time, and Dr.
King explains, "We did not take this radical step without
prolonged and prayerful consideration." After stating the reasons which led him and his associates—who had hitherto appealed for compliance with Supreme Court decisions and
federal rulings—to consider this tactic, Dr. King concludes:
"We decided, therefore, knowing well what the consequences
would be and prepared to accept them, that we had no choice
but to violate such an injunction." [1]

Clearly this occasion marked a watershed in the thinking
and strategy of Martin Luther King. But it was only a development of the tension with laws and legal processes which
had been felt by the civil rights movement from its beginning.
Through the late 1940's and early 1950's actions were brought
in courts (often by the legal services of the N.A.A.C.P.) which
led to decisions and federal orders that significantly reduced gov-
ernment-supported racial segregation. Laws were often the
occasion of the initial protest, but ultimately law was an

1

ally—albeit maddeningly slow moving. The Montgomery, Alabama, bus boycott began when, on December 5, 1955, Mrs.
Rosa Parks violated a local ordinance on segregated bus seating.
Thereafter, however, the boycott continued as a disciplined,
nonviolent campaign to induce the business and political powers of Montgomery to bring about change voluntarily. Through
the next two years, emphasis was on integrating public schools,
culminating in the confrontation at Little Rock, Arkansas, in
the fall of 1957. But on this issue all the violence and defiance
of law were on the part of the white opposition. The sit-in
movement began in February, 1960, and spread very rapidly.
Over the next two years the segregation of lunch counters,
libraries, recreation facilities, and churches (and the Jim Crow
ordinances which established some such practices in law) were
tested by disobedience. Repeatedly the courts upheld the protesters, and the legalized segregation of public facilities gave
way. In the summer of 1961, a series of freedom rides met
with opposition and on occasion with mob attack. But these
rides were intended to test local compliance with existing desegregation orders. The law was on the side of the riders, and
ultimately local officials were required to guarantee their safety.
These events will suggest some of the background which led
Dr. King to attach the significance he did to the decision in
Birmingham to violate a court order. Previously, if local
ordinances were manifestly unjust or local or state officials
treated any challenge to prevailing custom as an impertinence,
courts would find for the disobedients when such laws or
officials were disobeyed. But if court injunctions were to become instruments to oppose or delay social justice, Dr. King
and his associates concluded that courts too would have to be
disobeyed.

This account indicates dates and occasions to which we may
well assign the contemporary re-emergence in American society
of civil disobedience as an action to which large numbers of
persons are driven in conscience—and as a topic of public

notice which thoughtful persons must discuss. But so much has happened since these beginnings that events from even the recent past seem already remote. Civil disobedience has continued as one of the tactics of protest against the race-structured character of the American community, north and south. It has been adopted on occasion by those protesting the nation's neglect of the poor. It has been used by some students as a weapon against the paternalism and the bureaucratic obtuseness of educational institutions. But it has become even more characteristically an instrument of those who oppose, on moral grounds, the American military involvement in Vietnam. Some persons practice noncompliance with those rules and laws which would compel them to take part in a war they believe is wrong. Others who are not themselves liable for military service will create whatever obstruction they can to express their opposition to the war itself and to compulsory participation in it by anyone at all. Those who practice civil disobedience in this cause can count on the weight of federal resources being thrown against them and on little help from courts. The action they oppose is an action of the national government itself; there is no higher political jurisdiction to which they can appeal. Although civil disobedience in such instances calls for unusual courage and entails a high likelihood of punishment, there are no signs of its diminishing.

Since civil disobedience has recently been used largely as a weapon of social protest, an initial distinction, obvious though it may be, might here be made explicit. Not all protest is civil disobedience. Much protest—including much that is vigorous and effective—is entirely within the law, and indeed, in the United States, is protected in principle by constitutional guarantees of freedom of speech, of assembly, and of the right to petition for redress of grievances. The term "civil disobedience" is only properly applied when a law is broken—as when persons refuse to use racially segregated facilities in a segregated way, or when a young man refuses to register for the draft, or when a demonstration is held for which a permit was withheld, or even when mothers block streets in order to secure a traffic light at an intersection. Such acts must be intentional. That is, they must be deliberately done to preserve the individual's (or the group's) own integrity and to make a public protest against identified wrong. In sum, the question of civil disobedience is not, "May individuals or groups demonstrate or petition for the correction of what they take to be injustices?" Clearly they may. The question is more specifically, "Does the individual have the right—or perhaps the duty—to disobey the law when his mind, his conscience or his religious faith tells him that the law is unjust?" [2]

Some, though by no means all, of those who have set themselves openly and dramatically against the community and its laws have done so on religious grounds. Members of the clergy and of religious orders are often conspicuous and newsworthy in such acts by reason of their garb and their articulateness. But acts of defiance of law—and their attendant cost—have brought together persons of many sorts. Negroes and whites have shared picket lines and prisons. Laymen have been at least as active as have clergymen—indeed, mutual recognition of humanity and courage has moderated the clericalism of the church-identified forces. Protest has brought together, across confessional lines, persons from nearly every important group in the Jewish and Christian communities. And most important of all, those acting on the basis of religious conscience have discovered a deep unity with those whose conscience is not similarly informed. Manifestly a large segment of the American religious community has felt itself in conscience committed to roles which incur the possibility and the risk of deliberate violation of laws.

Equally obviously, another segment of the American religious community recognizes no such commitment. Orally or in print, thoughtful persons declare themselves "shocked" or "deeply troubled" by a course of action which seems to set the community of faith in open conflict with the organized society. Most of those who express this instinctive rejection of conscientious disobedience of law specify some qualifications. That is, they speak of "almost any" law or conditions. They seem willing to grant that there might be some situations in which it would be defensible to break a law. Presumably, for example, if laws or rulings were to restrict freedom to worship, the religious community would close ranks and agree that government had overstepped its proper role and should be defied. But in the minds of many persons, we face nothing remotely like that now. [For them, the values and interests of American society and the values and interests of the Christian Church have traditionally been and still are so substantially congruent or complementary that it is inconceivable that civil disobedience might, in our time and our land, be a calling under God.]

Thus the Christian community is markedly divided. What seems to be self-evidently a Christian duty to some seems, equally self-evidently, wrong-headed to others. If there are those who are surprised that the church might support disobedience, there are others who are surprised that Christian people will acquiesce in an unjust, repressive community or fail to challenge legally supported moral outrage. A course which seems to some to be simply obedience to the will of God as the church has received the same can seem to others to be at best unwise and at worst seditious and a departure from Christian faith and duty in the only form they have been given to understand them. Brother is set against brother.

It is hard to see how the church could be anything other than divided. A search of the standard ethics books and of the resources of theological libraries would indicate that a thorough, readily available discussion of Christian civil disobedience does not exist. Ignorance, misunderstanding, and division could have prevailed even if responsible ethical analyses had been abundant, of course. But they could hardly do anything but flourish when the subject has simply not been discussed. This crisis of conscience has taken too many people by surprise.

Of course, civil disobedience is not primarily a topic for discussion; it is an action, a commitment. It is something to be done or not done. Persons of conscience act because they must. Theory, in a sense, is secondary. But Christian commitment ought not to be impulsive or capricious. A fully human action must involve an understanding as well as a doing. It might be hoped that a commitment informed by rigorous thought would be better able to consider its own consequences, would take account of a wider range of reality, would be more sharable by a community of commitment, would have more clearly defined purposes, and would achieve more durable results than would a commitment made without reflection. The actions of Christian persons ought to be informed, sustained, and corrected by the kind of continuing ethical discourse which has been available on many subjects—but not on civil disobedience.

Since the 1930's, the Christian critique of social, political, and economic orders in this country retained sufficient confidence in the resilience and essential humaneness of American political institutions so that it was not necessary to consider a strategy and theory of disobedience. But now history (and behind that, the Lord of history) has placed the issue on the agenda of the church and the society. Some extended re-investigation of the conflict and the sources for thinking about it seems urgent.

A CASE AGAINST CIVIL DISOBEDIENCE

An analysis might well begin by taking account of the considerations which weigh against a course of civil disobedience. If this case is seldom articulated systematically it is not because some considerable arguments cannot be marshaled on its behalf. Anything which may be said in favor of civil disobedience must reckon with the real cogency and include the real insights of the opposition.

To put strongest matters first, those who would argue against the legitimacy for Christians (at least in the present setting) of a course of civil disobedience will appeal to the social necessity of law and order. For a society to survive, for it to pursue any common productive purposes, for it to maintain even minimal freedom and justice for the individual, it must be an ordered society. Have those who counsel noncompliance and who "take to the streets" considered the seriousness of a challenge to order and authority? If no one is bound by a law he chooses to regard as unjust, is not each person his own law? In other words, is not this doctrine actually the introduction of anarchy? The defenders of civil disobedience, it is contended, ought to realize that their opinion and conduct strike at the very heart of government itself.

In support of this argument, it is possible to cite weighty authority. St. Paul's teaching in Romans 13:1–2 is certain to be mentioned. The passage is unqualified in its claim for "civil obedience." "Let every person be subject to the governing authorities. For there is no authority except from God, and those that exist have been instituted by God. Therefore he who resists the authorities resists what God has appointed, and those who resist will incur judgment." These sentences (and the rest of the paragraph through verse 7) are the most full and explicit remarks in the New Testament concerning Christian duty to civil government, and taking them as they stand it would be very difficult to find in their terms anything which would sanction disobedience. Moreover, there are other portions of the New Testament which support this key passage. Christians are to "be subject for the Lord's sake to every human institution" (I Peter 2:13); they are to pay taxes (Romans 13:6–7), to pray for those in authority (I Timothy 2:1–2), to honor the emperor (I Peter 2:17), and to live peaceably with all (Romans 12:18). This is hardly a program for insurrectionists.

Christian thought has developed these biblical hints in two

distinguishable traditions of theory of the state. One succession of spokesmen traces from Augustine through Luther and Calvin to Reinhold Niebuhr. The representatives of this succession differ among themselves in emphasis and idiom, of course, and their opinions on the specific issue of civil disobedience might be quite divergent. But, by and large, they agree in stressing the sinfulness of man and the providential institution of government as a restraint on man's rapacity and selfishness. (This "Augustinian" emphasis on man's ineradicable sinfulness and the consequent necessity of the state was anticipated in the Stoic, Seneca, and it has continued to find congenial place in the thinking of some who are not explicitly Christian. A secularized version of the theme appears in Thomas Hobbes, and, indeed, it underlies the interpretation of constitutional theory in *The Federalist Papers*.) Order and peace are very great goods. They are gifts of God—granted and maintained through the structures of authority and justice (admittedly imperfect) which civil government provides.

Another tradition of Christian thought, pursuing an Aristotelian influence, can be identified in Thomas Aquinas, Richard Hooker, Jacques Maritain, and John Courtney Murray—to cite only a few representative names. This tradition is less inclined to stress man's sin and its destructive potential but more inclined to stress the positive purposes for which society exists and the role of government in furthering, or at least in providing the precondition for the pursuit of, these purposes. These beneficent ends and government as a means to them are by God's appointment in the natural order.

These massive traditions agree that the Christian has a stake in the maintenance of civil order and that there is a great deal which is properly due unto Caesar.

Defenders of this line of argument have not supposed that human government is perfect. Some writers have explicitly urged that obedience should be given even to those rulers who are guilty of grave injustice. Not all rulers are good, but all are ordained of God, and God has his purposes in a defective regime to which it is a Christian's duty to submit in patience. St. Gregory, for example, counseled that if the people observed faults in their rulers, "they wax not bold against them" but, rather, that they consider the matter inwardly "that constrained by the fear of God, they refuse not to bear the yoke of obedience under them." [3]

This general reverence for government, for law, for duly constituted authority, and for social order is undoubtedly the strongest substantive point that can be urged against a course of civil disobedience; and a great deal can be said on its behalf. But arguments of a more tactical nature also support the case.

The method widely used in civil disobedience is regarded as questionable. Civil disobedience has, in the present situation, created an alliance with nonviolent resistance. (The alliance is not maintained equally by all proponents of civil disobedience nor exercised in the same form by all who use it, but by many the stratagem and the method are closely bound together.) Indeed, a mystique has gathered around the nonviolent method— drawing some power from continued associations with the moral force of Gandhi. Defenders of civil disobedience seem, to their opponents, to risk deifying nonviolent resistance.

These opponents find the mystique unpersuasive. It is maintained, on high moral grounds, that those who practice nonviolent resistance honor the law by disobeying it and paying the required penalty. But the counter-argument asks: Is not this contention just a juggling with words? One honors the law by obeying it. Law is not something to be trifled with in this way. In an eloquent article, George F. Kennan has said:

The violation of law is not, in the moral and philosophic sense, a privilege that lies offered for sale with a given price tag, like an object in a supermarket, available to anyone who has the price and is willing to pay for it. It is not like the privilege of breaking crockery in a tent at the county fair for a quarter a shot. Respect for the law is not an obligation which is exhausted or obliterated by willingness to accept the penalty for breaking it.

To hold otherwise would be to place the privilege of lawbreaking preferentially in the hands of the affluent, to make respect for law a commercial proposition rather than a civic duty and to deny any authority of law independent of the sanctions established against its violation. It would then be all right for a man to create false fire alarms or frivolously to pull the emergency cord on the train, or to do any number of other things that endangered or inconvenienced other people, provided only he was prepared to accept the penalties of so doing. Surely, lawlessness and civil disobedience cannot be condoned or tolerated on this ground.[4]

If one claims to be honoring the law, let him go about it in a less devious and morally questionable way.

The timing and wisdom in the current practice of civil disobedience are similarly questioned. There are those who grant hypothetically that civil disobedience can be an allowable Christian action, but they contend that this is neither the time nor the place to put it into practice. These are unsettled times. Many communities are filled with agitation and unrest and some with open rioting. Community order is a very fragile and precious thing. It is secured only by generations of hard-won gains; and it can be undone very rapidly. Such considerations call for restraint, moderation, and a reaffirmation of the moral sanctions for obedience. The self-assertive spirit of disorder is abroad. Forces are present that could reduce community to chaos. Hence, it is widely felt, regardless of theoretical considerations, this is not the time to encourage apparent lawlessness. Christians ought to throw their weight on the side of law and constituted authority. Community leaders ought to be able to look to the churches for statements and actions which will reinforce rather than endanger the human community. If there must be change, let it be gradual and peaceful; our flexible political institutions allow such. But civil disobedience is too disruptive; it is a means out of harmony with any end that can in these tense days be regarded as defensible.

Perhaps these arguments cover the ground, at least in outline. They may suggest the points that are urged against civil disobedience and suggest as well that the case has genuine force. Behind the arguments are some important insights and affirmations which deliver the case from moral shallowness. Civil disobedience is not opposed on the basis of mere prudential caution. Those who oppose civil disobedience do so because they understand the importance—indeed, the indispensability—of an ordered community, and they affirm the sanctity of law as the bond of that order.

LOCATING THE ISSUE

These affirmations are valuable, but they are not in dispute. They are a common ingredient of any responsible theorizing about the nature of community. They would be stated in not radically dissimilar terms by Roy Wilkins and Governor Ronald Reagan and cherished alike by the editors of *Christianity and Crisis* and of *Christian Economics*.

There are, of course, in American society today groups which recognize little or no stake in public order. There are those who, with an extreme sense of alienation, in effect secede from the society. There are those who, expressing their nihilism and sense of exile, are prepared to riot and destroy. There are those who, informed by more or less explicit doctrine, are commending revolution. All these groups will use the ordered society when it serves them, but they feel no loyalty to it and no stake in its survival. These "outsider" groups are a rebuke and a concern to the whole community which is held in unified discourse by the common recognition of the necessity of law. All these groups are alike in their readiness to disregard civil law as it suits their purposes to do so. Their style of challenge to the conventional, established community requires discussion in any large consideration of civil disobedience. Chapter Eight of this book examines that disobedience to law which aims at the radical reconstruction of the community and the destruction of the present order.

But most of those persons, now and in the past, who have raised the issue of civil disobedience have intended by their dissent to affirm the essential order of their communities. They were and are driven to disobey their communities as they are, out of loyalty to them as they are convinced they might become. The greater portion of this book is devoted to civil disobedience of this sort—civil disobedience which is not revolt.

Anyone who opposes civil disobedience categorically is unlikely to recognize such a distinction. For him, the rioter, the dissenter, the moralist—all, insofar as they engage in or defend lawbreaking, are of the same spirit. All deserve the community's condemnation for law violations they commit or condone. Lawbreaking is lawbreaking, and that is an end to the matter. The breakers of civil law may be acknowledged to differ in their style and in the kinds and amounts of damage they inflict. But these are seen as difference in degree among those who share the same basic error of disrespect for law.

So the argument would have it. But those who practice or defend civil disobedience as distinguished from rebellion would insist that a distinction in kind is involved. A human act takes its meaning from the context of large purposes in which it is carried out. A handshake made as a gesture of agreement and trust is one thing. A handshake between a confidence artist and his victim is another. Similarly, the argument goes, one must take account of the intentions of the persons involved before he can judge the quality of a specific act of lawbreaking. The pictures in the newspapers (usually showing arrests) might look deceptively alike, but one law violation can be quite different from another. It would be a strangely brittle, legalistic mind which would see all laws as having the same crucial significance and all violations as constituting the same threat and deserving the same condemnation with no further questions asked.

Those who defend the possibility of responsible civil disobedience and who do so in a context of loyalty to the true order of the community would reject the notion that their violations of the law are just the opening end of a breakdown of which riot and revolt are the developed expressions. Quite on the contrary, they would think of their own effort as directly *opposed to* and intended as a *preventive of* riot and revolt. In a complacent society, civil disobedience, by calling urgent attention to social ills and achieving some relief, may be one of the community's aids against violence and revolution. Civil disobedience can be a tool in the hands of responsible citizens who, having a stake in the ordered society, determine to remove those grievances which, unmet, tend inevitably to produce riot and revolt. In the light of their intentions, civil disobedience and rebellion may not be different stages of the same thing; they may be opposing forces.

These persons who, having a loyalty to the ordered community of which they are part, yet feel themselves compelled to entertain the possibility of, and actually to engage in, acts of civil disobedience would raise questions about these abstractions "law" and "order" to which such deference is paid. Just to affirm the value of order and the sanctity of law does not illuminate the contemporary problem. The statements of a generalized piety are not pertinent to this specific crisis. Some further inquiry is required.

What is "order"? Is it "whatever is"? How is order achieved? The processes observable would suggest that community order is the result of reconciling—more or less justly and permanently —the various forces of a pluralistic society. Order is not the serene, formal thing the word might seem to imply; it is dynamic and is created by the provisional resolution of deep tensions.

Similarly, what is "law"? Is it whatever positive regulations happen now to be in force? Is it the static reflection of rules written in the heavens that those—even Christians—who speak of its "sacredness" apparently take it to be? Is it a neat, interlocking system which is in peril as a whole when any part is questioned? Such questions could lead into a discussion of philosophies of law; but short of that, some common-sense observations sufficient for present purposes might be widely agreed to. A thing is not right because it is legal. All manner of inhumanity has been embodied in formally correct laws that have been acknowledged by the communities for which they were written. In his great "Letter from Birmingham Jail," Martin Luther King put undiscriminating deference to law in proper perspective by his reminder, "We should never forget that everything Adolf Hitler did in Germany was 'legal.' " [5] Formal and procedural correctness do not in themselves confer honor on a law which raises it above further question. Laws are written and enforced by persons of more or less ability and disinterestedness as an attempt to approximate that justice which the community ought to embody. Such an attempt is never more than partially successful; its inadequacies must be identified and remedied. Laws in the American system have not been written to conform to some consistent ideology; they are a mixed lot written rather pragmatically in response to felt needs under the general empowering and restraints of the Constitution. The community is not deeply threatened when this flexible body of laws undergoes the necessary self-correction. New events and new forces put new stresses on old structures. Hence, law is a growing, changing thing responding to new insights and unprecedented occurrences.

A general appeal to law and order assumes that calm and outward order in the community constitute the supreme civic good—as though there were no difference between the calm of justice and contentment and the calm of tyranny and repression. The same appeal assumes that all disorder and challenge to authority is evil—as though the community did not grow by the resolution of conflict.

The present situation does not pose for the responsible citizen the academic questions: Is law a good thing? or, Is order better than disorder? Self-evidently they are.

The present situation poses much more specific and difficult questions:

What should one do in the face of unjust laws? Sometimes a stubbornly maintained state law or local ordinance is patently in conflict with a federal law or with a court interpretation of the Constitution. Sometimes a law may be so openly discriminatory that to obey it would demean one's own sense of humanity and personal worth. Sometimes even federal regulations can, in the opinion of some citizens, so violate the American axioms of "life, liberty, and the pursuit of happiness" that they are actually agents of death, oppression, and the perpetuation of misery. In such cases—whether the appeal is to a federal norm, to the American ideal, to "a decent respect for the opinions of mankind," or to an ultimate moral order—law is in conflict with law. It is not a question of "Should the law be obeyed?" but of "Which law should be obeyed?" Disorder is not injected into society by those who challenge unjust laws, but by those who write and enforce them. When, in a society professing a dedication to justice, unjust laws are maintained, the society is in a state of moral confusion. Those who use whatever means seem necessary to draw attention to the situation do not create the disorder; they simply identify and refuse to cooperate in the disorder which is already there.

Similarly: What part of my government am I to obey? Who determines for me just what the law is? In a checks-and-balances system, the courts have often reversed legislatures and upset administrative procedures. Then they too have been denounced and their determinations said by offended legislators not to be "the law of the land." Courts are, of course, not infallible; they have reversed themselves. But their personnel is of a generally superior sort; they are usually less vulnerable to political influence; they act with a greater sense of a humane tradition, more disciplined procedures, and a deeper scrutiny of the issues; the higher courts are less dominated by regional or local passion than are town councils and state legislatures. Hence, persons discriminated against have often found the courts to be their ally against legislative and executive abuse of power. The process is slow, and initial appeals to courts in issues which were ultimately vindicated were often rebuffed. Courts, as a rule, are happier with minimal rulings than with sweeping decisions. Yet the courts have been, by and large, a dependable guarantor of rights and liberties.[6] However, issues do not come before courts just because they ought to be reviewed by some relatively dispassionate body. Courts do not consider a local, state, or national law, nor any executive regulation or procedure, until it is challenged. If a group is persuaded that a law is unjust and that a court would so determine and if the law is not one on which there has been a previous ruling, the issue can be brought into the courts only by a violation of the law in question. Unless the process begins with disobedience, there can be no judicial relief from a legislature determined to keep an oppressive law on the books or an executive determined to give such a law active enforcement. Intentional disobedience against one branch of government may be the only way to appeal to another. Indeed, the disobedience may need to be rather dramatic and widespread in order to get the cumbersome machinery of the court system to take notice rapidly enough to be of help to this generation rather than only to the next.

What should one do when laws are unequally and oppressively enforced? There is a substantial portion of American society whose experience has given it no occasion to question seriously the essential adequacy, fairness, and impartiality of our lawmaking, enforcing, and adjudicating procedures. Many citizens have learned from childhood a comfortable, middle-class respect for the police and for officialdom in general—a respect which the conduct in office of many public officials does much to justify. But other portions of American society have, from childhood, had frequent occasion to question all these things. They think of the processes of government as created by and serving the interests of others and as invariably set against themselves. Suspicion, arrest, conviction, and sentencing seem to fall differently on "us" and on "them." Rights and protections (and evasions) are available to "them" that "we" have no access to. There seems to be a malign arbitrariness in the exercise of that power of which the police are the principal symbol and instrument. Hence, questions must be raised by the community about those persons whose roles put them at the meeting place of the power of the system and the relative weakness of the disadvantaged individual. Whence are policemen recruited? How are they trained? Who employs them and directs their work? What checks are there against the quite understandable tendency of officers to overreact under pressure? What training or regulation restrains the power of police to use for the expression of personal, race, or class prejudice the margin of initiative and personal judgment they must have in their work? To whom are the police answerable? What impartial appeal is possible for a citizen who supposes himself to have been treated by the police with less than even-handed justice? What interests do the holders of minor judiciary posts instinctively favor, and what interests do they instinctively fail to recognize? Who sit on draft boards, and what collective bias are they likely to represent? The unhappy fact is that the structures of government which are meant to serve and protect the proper interests of all can become —and unless checked will almost inevitably become—captive of some dominant portion of the society. A part of the community—often a part with narrow vision and attracted by power—can seize the structures of government, including the quite terrifying apparatus of force and compulsion, and use them for the furtherance of its own purposes and the repression of those it chooses to repress. Instead of being the defender and guarantor of the rights of all, especially of the weak, the government itself becomes the oppressor. Examples are abundant. An advisory committee passed on to the U.S. Civil Rights Commission in February of 1965 a report concluding that Negroes in Mississippi live in a state of terror due in part to an apparent "pattern of collusion between local law enforcement officers and hoodlum elements." [7] In such a situation, the life, property, and essential humanity of all citizens as well as the dignity of government have been cheapened. Lawlessness has become legalized. But such examples are not confined to one section of the country or to one issue. John C. Bennett recently commented on the role of the police in the disturbances at Columbia University:

When the police first invaded the campus on April 30 the degree of their violence took both students and faculty by surprise. They went against the instructions of the university administration, which had told them to carry no weapons into the buildings and to limit their activities to the clearing of the buildings. Much of the trouble came when they proceeded to clear the entire campus of hundreds of students and faculty. In so doing they backed many of them against fences and clubbed them while they drove others through the gate with their horses. These things had to be seen to be believed. Readers who have had neither first- nor second-hand contact with these events cannot be expected to understand the range of the solidarity in the Columbia community created by the police "bust." What does a society do when its instrument for maintaining external order becomes itself a source of deeper disorder? [8]

Again, when arbitrary rulings and officials are defied in conscience, the defiance does not introduce disrespect and caprice into the orderly workings of a municipality. Rather, such a challenge may be an attempt to bring some measure of honor and responsibility into a situation in which cynicism, contempt for persons, and misuse of public trust have prevailed unchecked.

What course is open when the normal means of petition for redress of grievances are not available? The American system assumes that officials, the laws they write, and their conduct in office are answerable to the electorate. Further, when government seems unresponsive to the needs of portions of the community, the Constitution guarantees that a wronged group can make representation of its cause—with the clear implication that it is the duty of government to heed insofar as equal justice allows. The rights of the few, the weak, and the voiceless are as important as are the rights of the many, the powerful, and the articulate. But, in practice, this process gets cut off. In some cases, the failure is due to the arrogance of government officials. *New York Times* reporter Anthony Lewis gives the following account:

> On September 19, 1963, twelve Negro residents of Clinton, Louisiana, wrote letters to the mayor and the district attorney requesting the appointment of a bi-racial committee on community relations. They suggested respectfully that such a committee could give "careful consideration of the many problems facing our community" and would help "to avoid civil domestic disturbances of racial tension." One of the writers was a seventy-five-year-old woman, a lifelong resident of the area; another was the husband of the superintendent of the local Negro schools.
>
> The response came on December 3rd, when the twelve Negroes were arrested. . . .[9]

The case is far from isolated. But the normal interaction between government and people can be shut off in other ways. In many communities, minority groups have been systematically (and by the use of intimidation) excluded from voting. Elsewhere, rootless groups, such as migrant farm workers, are without vote and sympathetic representation. Or the very poor and the ill-educated have a vote so controlled as not to constitute a responsible participation in democratic process. One large and important group, the nation's youth, are similarly without effective political voice. Those aged eighteen to twenty-one may be asked to fight in behalf of policies and causes which they have not a citizen's role in shaping. Even those who are over twenty-one are likely (given the widening gap between the generations) to regard their point of view as very ill-represented and their interests as all but disregarded. Many in the younger generation voice a sense of futility about politics—not about one party or even both, but about the process itself.

The conviction is widespread that lawmaking is largely under the control of dominant economic powers and is used for their purposes in disregard of public welfare. The wishes of groups with specialized interests and money to have them represented can be spoken for by lobbyists skilled at the art of influencing legislation. But what can be done by those who have only their bodies and their voices and yet feel that their just demands have gone unheeded? Henry Steele Commager's remarks about student protests might apply more widely:

> Businessmen and doctors and lawyers, to be sure, funnel their protests through respectable organizations like chambers of commerce, or the American Medical Association, or the American and state bar associations, or resort to well-paid lobbyists to express their discontent; students have no such effective organizations nor can they support lobbying. To penalize them for their weakness and their poverty is to repeat the error of the Cleveland administration in arresting Coxey's Army for walking on the grass or of the Hoover administration in sending soldiers to destroy the pitiful Bonus Army. The rich and respectable have always had their ways of making their discontent heard; the poor and the unorganized must resort to protests and marches and demonstrations.[10]

When substantial groups of citizens feel that nothing they can do or say—following the accepted rules—will have the slightest effect on the course of government, that no argument they advance will be answered on its merits, that their representation of what they take to be a just cause will be met with contempt, they are led, in despair, to work outside the conventional, peaceful patterns. Direct action, not discussion; civil disobedience, not conformity, seen the best courses open to make some impact on a society whose political processes have excluded them.

To summarize, the pieties about the value of law and order

might be a sufficient answer to civil disobedience if one could assume a society in which just laws were fairly administered and in which a responsive government kept short accounts with the needs of all its people letting required changes take place frequently, peacefully, and gradually. But precedents drawn up for some such ideal situation will not do for significant portions of American society as it is. We are faced with a community which in many places and in important areas of its life is a community gone wrong. The stresses on those who seek to act responsibly in such a situation are very great. Extreme sickness may call forth drastic remedies.

two
: :
THE NEW TESTAMENT
ON THE STATE

The argument against civil disobedience sketched in the foregoing chapter has already introduced biblical material. But a more careful examination seems desirable. It may be that considerations of biblical authority do not weigh heavily among those who are deciding to obey or not to obey the law. John C. Bennett recently expressed an opinion that in our time scriptural citations "have largely lost their power as a law binding the consciences of Christians." [1] He is probably correct. Yet throughout the discussion of civil disobedience, in the Christian community, references continue to be made to biblical teaching and precedent. Probably few Christians would feel comfortable in an ethical position which could demonstrate no rootage in the New Testament; and most Christians will recognize a necessity to examine contemporary problems, especially one as important as civil disobedience, in the light of that literature which has been continuously validated as testimony to the acts and purposes of God.

But such examination is not a matter of quoting texts or eliciting permanent principles. In ancient events, God acted in judgment and grace, and man responded in rejection or obedience. But the character both of God's self-revelation and of man's response was determined by the situation—a situation specific and unique in each case, and in every case different in important respects from any contemporary situation. Yet the God who revealed his character and purposes—revealed them

22

in many times and ways, but supremely in Jesus Christ—is the same then as now; his basic will for man is unchanged. So the task of anyone who would cite biblical authority is to ask: Knowing (insofar as we do) what the faith community understood to be the will of God in its situation in the past, what can we responsibly take the will of God to be for us in our very different situation?

THE NEW TESTAMENT "YES" TO THE STATE

With this methodological assumption made explicit, the biblical material requires examination, and we might begin with a further look at a passage which has already been mentioned, Romans 13:1-7:*

Let every person be subject to the governing authorities. For there is no authority except from God, and those that exist have been instituted by God. Therefore he who resists the authorities resists what God has appointed, and those who resist will incur judgment. For rulers are not a terror to good conduct, but to bad. Would you have no fear of him who is in authority? Then do what is good, and you will receive his approval, for he is God's servant for your good. But if you do wrong, be afraid, for he does not bear the sword in vain; he is the servant of God to execute his wrath on the wrongdoer. Therefore one must be subject, not only to avoid God's wrath but also for the sake of conscience. For the same reason you also pay taxes, for the authorities are ministers of God attending to this very thing. Pay all of them their dues, taxes to whom taxes are due, revenue to whom revenue is due, respect to whom respect is due, honor to whom honor is due.

This passage is, to repeat, the most extended and the most positive discussion anywhere in the New Testament of Christian duty to civil government. St. Paul counsels that all authority is of God—an idea clearly derivable from the Old Testament

* Scripture quotations are from the Revised Standard Version unless otherwise specified.

(Daniel 4:28ff., cf. Wisdom of Solomon 6:1–3) and reflected in contemporary Jewish opinion (Josephus, *Jewish War,* II, 140, "No ruler attains his office save by the will of God"). Therefore, a Christian is, positively, to obey the governing authorities and, negatively, not to resist them—lest, in resisting them, he resist what God has appointed. In support of this contention, St. Paul urges that governments are a terror to those who do evil works. Those who do good have nothing to fear from the authorities, but those who do evil can expect that, in the providential ordering of things, government will be a "servant of God" to execute his "wrath" on those who have violated their due. Since government is appointed to this important role of approving good and punishing evil, it should be given fitting honor and respect. But even more, it should be granted, for conscience' sake, the participation and self-investment which taxes represent. (This was written at a time when taxes were burdensome and widely resented in the provinces.)

In order to estimate this passage rightly, its setting must be borne in mind. Admittedly some conjecture is required; commentators note the abruptness with which the topic is introduced and the scarcity of clues as to its intention. The flat, unqualified terms St. Paul uses here have suggested to interpreters that some Christians in the first century (the "you" of the passage) supposed that their faith released them from all obligation to civil authority. Perhaps some were reproducing in the Christian community the rejection of pagan government characteristic of radical Jewish opinion. Perhaps some were taking their liberty in Christ—as "the Lord's freeman" (I Corinthians 7:22)—in so uncriticized a sense as to make them contemptuous of all governmental obligation. In any case, a strong statement was called for.

These Pauline injunctions about civil government are not as unqualified as they may at first seem. They are part of a lengthy, connected conclusion to the epistle setting forth the ethic of the new age. St. Paul's appeal begins by urging that the whole of life is offered to God in view of God's mercy in Christ; it is being transformed toward the perfect will of God (12:1f.). Moreover, it is a shared life full of mutual obligations among brothers (12:3–13). It is a life whose every contact with those outside the fellowship must be expressive of love —love which refuses to take vengeance into its own hands (12:14–21). The love by which a Christian lives is not against law, but it is the fulfillment of moral law (13:8–10). The whole community in Christ lives in expectation of the return of its Lord and conducts itself in the joy and discipline of those who, in the midst of darkness, know the light is breaking (13:11–14). Taking account of this context, it might be possible to paraphrase St. Paul's thought in Romans 13:1–7 rather like this: "Christ, the Lord to whom we owe everything, will return. The time is short. Meantime, you already conduct yourselves by a love which transcends legalism. But this transitoriness of the present age and this higher practice of love beyond law are not reasons for disrespect for authorities. The government and its agents have been instituted by God and serve his purposes. The Roman empire (even under Nero) gives order to the world which allows the gospel to be preached. It is an ally—doing its proper duty of repressing evil and encouraging good. It should not be opposed." At the time of this epistle, St. Paul's experience would have confirmed this teaching. He had been able to plead his Roman citizenship to some advantage to the gospel. His opposition had come mainly from Jewish enemies. The empire had been a restraint on persecution.

This passage from Romans, important though it is, should not be universalized. It was not St. Paul's intention to lay down a law good for all Christians at all times and all places. We cannot justly use a fragment of this letter to answer directly questions which arise out of other settings. From this passage alone, we do not know what St. Paul would have said a few years later when Domitian declared himself *Deus et dominus*

or two centuries later when Diocletian outlawed the church. Still less do we know what he would say in a modern situation in which a government had manifestly become an agent of terror, not to evil works, but to people seeking basic human rights. Even though there is no clear way of knowing, it seems likely that such situations would introduce qualifying considerations, not present when St. Paul wrote to Rome about A.D. 55, in the light of which he might modify his statement on Christian duty to government. In any case, it seems certain that the apostle who began his ethical section with "Do not be conformed to this world" would resist having his comments in chapter 13 taken to mean unquestioning assent to the state. Paul, as a man in Christ, could never say, "My government right or wrong." If this passage has been, as Dr. Bennett contends, "the proof text to support despotism and to discourage revolution and civil disobedience in every period and many traditions," [2] it has, in the process, been wrested into contexts for which it was not written and to which it is not truly apposite.

One aspect of the primitive Christian Yes to the state is implicit in the vocabulary of this passage in Romans. St. Paul, in speaking of the officials of government conducting their quite ordinary civic functions, uses cultic terms—terms which he uses elsewhere to designate some of the central ministries within the Christian fellowship. G. W. H. Lampe has put the matter this way:

The emperor is God's *diaconos,* either for good or as an executor of divine wrath. The officers of the State are *leitourgoi theou.* The use of these Christian and, indeed, liturgical, words to describe the secular rulers of a heathen empire is, to my mind, very impressive. . . . The idea that the emperor and his governors are actually ministers and officiants of the service of God means that God is truly the Lord of the world and that service is rendered to him quite outside the boundaries of the Church and even by those who do not acknowledge him.[3]

Other passages supplement the Yes of Romans usefully.

I Peter 2:13–17 commends honor to the emperor "for the Lord's sake." Titus 3:1 exhorts Christians "to be submissive to rulers and authorities" and "to be obedient." And I Timothy 2:1–2 urges "that supplications, prayers, intercessions, and thanksgivings be made for all men, for kings and for all who are in high positions, that we may lead a quiet and peaceable life, godly and respectful in every way." This prayer for those in authority was not a perfunctory thing. A New Testament scholar has commented:

> The Church must bless God that he has blessed the work of Caesar. She must thank God for the *pax Augusti*. She must be the intercessor for the authorities of the State. For that is the most distinctive, and sometimes the only, thing that the Church can do in politics, viz. to intercede for the civil powers before God. She intercedes, says the martyr Justin, even when the State despises her prayer. Indeed, then the Church prays aright for the first time, since it is then that the authorities have most need of the intercessions of the Church.[4]

From these brief New Testament passages, a point of view emerges—at least fragmentarily. God rules all. He rules through his ordered creation. In the state there are those who bear rule as his ministers, and there are those who are subjects. (Similarly, in the tables of mutual obligations which recur in the New Testament, the family is hierarchical with husbands ruling wives, parents ruling children, and owners ruling slaves. The church too, in the New Testament literature, assumes the characteristics of an ordered community.) The prerogatives of governors are manifestations of a providential moral rule—a terror to evil works and an encouragement to good. Resistance to these rulers is a profound rebellion against the God by whom the "powers that be" are established. The appropriate attitude of a subject is submission. For conscience' sake, a Christian citizen is to obey the authorities, to seek the approval of rulers by doing good, to pay taxes, to give respect and honor where they are due, and to offer thanksgiving and intercession for those who bear rule. In sum, Christians are to submit themselves to every institution of man for the Lord's sake. The New Testament (showing some general kinship with Stoicism) gives this undeniable Yes to civil government and affirms it on the highest grounds.

THE NEW TESTAMENT "NO" TO THE STATE

But that is not the whole of the evidence, for the same New Testament contains an equally emphatic No. The hierarchy is not as it should be. The "powers" are in revolt. There is an ambivalence in the primitive Christian attitude toward civil government, and the evidence for the negative needs now to be considered.

One interesting line of argument deserves examination even though it has not commended itself equally to all New Testament scholars. In Romans 13, St. Paul speaks of government as "the powers that be." The term "powers" takes on a quasi-technical force in Paul's vocabulary. It has been thought productive to set the term in Romans 13 in the context of the broad Pauline conception of "principalities and powers." The Romans passage is positive in its attitude toward the "powers"; they are established by God and are his ministers for the service of men. The rest of Pauline usage is negative. The New Testament seems largely to suppose that neither man nor his institutions rule themselves. The affairs of history are aspects of a cosmic warfare (Ephesians 6:12). The nations have their angel-princes (Daniel 10:20, et al.). It is in terms of these "powers" that St. Paul concludes that the rulers of the world are set against God. He remarks, "None of the rulers of this age understood" the purposes of God, "for if they had, they would not have crucified the Lord of glory" (I Corinthians 2:8). The antagonism against God of the ruling forces of the old age is most clearly dramatized, St. Paul contends, in the crucifixion of Jesus. At the place where God was most openly manifest in history, the opposition to him of the organized structures of man's life was most openly evoked.

The "powers" are not a totally alien order; they are part of the one creation. Indeed, Colossians 1:16 speaks of them as "created in Christ." They have their properly appointed role in the providential ordering of the cosmos. But these "powers" are now enemies and alien to God's purposes. The New Testament scheme of thought nowhere conjectures how this hostility came to be; it is simply assumed to be the case. But Christ's death and resurrection have a cosmic significance. The "powers" are now overcome in Christ. The weakness of the Cross has triumphed over them (Colossians 2:13–15; Ephesians 1:20–22). This triumph is not realized in history, but it is pledged in the end when Christ will render the whole fruit of his triumph to the Father (I Corinthians 15:20–28). Thus, for St. Paul, the cosmos, the "powers" of heaven and earth, and the life of man are bound up together. They are made in Christ; they are now in sin; they are redeemed in Christ; they will be claimed by their Lord.

Not all New Testament scholars are willing to regard this circle of Pauline ideas as a legitimate part of the interpretation of Romans 13. It is held that the term "powers" there has no necessary connection with the "powers of this world" which figure in the quasi-mythical strain of Pauline thought just sketched. The thesis that the two ideas are to be linked at Romans 13 is most closely associated with the name and advocacy of Oscar Cullmann,[5] and this position has commended itself widely in Anglo-Saxon scholarship. But the rejection of Cullmann's thesis has prevailed among German critics.[6] It does seem, however, that for purposes of this argument it is not important whether or not the Pauline concept of the "powers" is to be read in the language of Romans 13. Whether it is or not, the theme of the "powers" in its own right presents a powerful New Testament idea in which the affairs of men and nations are depicted as on a course opposed to God and his purposes. The "powers" need have no ultimate terror for a Christian who knows their revolt is broken (Romans 8:38f.). But their opposition continues. This theme is an aspect of the New Testament No to government. Behind the visible culture, religion, and politics of man's world are supra-human forces which frustrate God's intentions. Whatever the present-day Christian community may want to make of this early picture of the "powers," the image is a witness to the persistent sense of the unmanageability of history; a deceiving, dividing, dis-creative factor is present in human affairs.[7] One would have to be an exceedingly impercipient reader of world events today to write off the New Testament sense of the "powers" and their connection with the state. If the primitive myth seems dispensable in a scientific age, the analysis of the human condition to which it witnesses was never more pertinent.

Other features of the New Testament No can be briefly itemized. Perhaps the most eloquent and memorable No grows out of the early clash between the apostles and the ruling Sadducees. The apostles were arrested for preaching in the Temple, and when they were reminded of the strict charge they had been given on an earlier occasion "not to teach in this name," Peter and the apostles answered, "We must obey God rather than men" (Acts 5:29, cf. chapters 3–5). The passage draws a distinction; the voice of human authority is not here the voice of God but, rather, a voice of mere men raised against God. To disobey it is a holy obligation. Bishop Henson (no friend of sedition, one can be sure) once remarked:

It is surely significant that the first public utterance of the leaders of the Christian society when they were confronted by the Sanhedrin's prohibition, was the rebellious declaration, "We must obey God rather than men." Henceforward there could be no question for any Christian of a single allegiance. Always he had to make his count with two claimants to his obedience. His earthly citizenship would coexist with another and a higher.[8]

Earlier, in recounting the same incident, the evangelical No to the state and the prophetic sense of God's Lordship over the nations are combined in an eloquent prayer. Peter and John had been imprisoned and released. On rejoining their brothers, they prayed:

Sovereign Lord, who didst make the heaven and the earth and the sea and everything in them, who by the mouth of our father David, thy servant didst say by the Holy Spirit,

"Why did the Gentile rage,
and the peoples imagine vain things?
The kings of the earth set themselves in array,
and the rulers were gathered together,
against the Lord and against his Anointed"—

for truly in this city there were gathered together against thy holy servant Jesus, whom thou didst anoint, both Herod and Pontius Pilate, with the Gentiles and the peoples of Israel, to do whatever thy hand and thy plan had predestined to take place. . . .

Acts 4:24–28, cf.24–30

The nations and their rulers conspire *against* the Lord and his Christ. But, despite their intent, he is creator and ruler of all, and turns the wrath of men to the accomplishment of his purposes. His will is a restraint on the ability of nations to persist and succeed in evil. But, if the nations are God's servants, they are his unwilling servants. They are depicted in this thunderous No passage as a coalition of God's enemies.

In the opening verses of I Corinthians 6, Christians are forbidden to bring their disputes into courts of law. Quarrels are to be settled within the church. In this passage, Paul regards the state, in its central business of the administration of justice, as without competence in issues involving the people of God.

The most dramatic No to the state in the New Testament literature in found in the Apocalypse. The opposition between a tyrannous government making absolute, divine claims, on the one side, and God and his people, on the other—an opposition hinted at in several of the later New Testament books—reaches a climax in Revelation 13. The beast ("monster" in one recent commentary) certainly refers to the Roman empire. But behind the power of the beast is the dragon, identified in the previous chapter as the devil, Satan, the deceiver who fought against Michael and his angels in a war in heaven. To the beast, "the dragon gave his power and his throne and great authority" (verse 2). This idea of a regime whose authority is given by the devil is the polar opposite of the language of Romans 13: "The powers that be are ordained of God." The beast is linked with a second beast which makes all the world render worship to the first beast and performs marvels to reinforce these deceitful claims to homage. The state, in this picture, is arrogant, oppressive, universal; and it exacts the worship of men. The state "claims for Caesar the things that are God's." [9] The empire is set radically against God; but it does him the honor of mimicry. Expositors have noted in the imagery of evil powers here imitations of the Trinity, the incarnation, the resurrection, and a Universal Church.[10] The conflict is dreadful for those who would be faithful. The beast utters haughty and blasphemous words against God. It makes war on the saints and conquers them. Those who will not worship the image of the beast are slain. "Here is a call for the endurance and faith of the saints." The imagery describes a malign, all-powerful, spiritual-political reality of which the early church—and many generations since— had intimate acquaintance.

These brief comments will have suggested that the New Testament literature sets a strong No to the state alongside its strong Yes.[11]

THE NEW TESTAMENT "PERHAPS" TO THE STATE

But the New Testament seems to have another thread which is not No and not Yes, but more qualified. It might be called the New Testament Perhaps to the state.[12]

The background for this more conditional attitude lies in the Old Testament prophets. They insist that God has called Israel and bound this people into the fulfillment of his purposes. But they also speak of his call of other nations and even of an exodus which he made for them as he had for Israel (Amos 9:7). The prophets know that God can make other enemy nations his instruments against his own people (Isaiah 10:5–6; Habakkuk 1:6ff.). The Hebrews and the other nations are judged alike for their sins (Amos 1 and 2), and a blessing is promised to all alike (Isaiah 19:24f.). In other words, for the prophets, God is Lord of all people and nations, and he works out his purposes in world history. But no one may presume to know his ways. As soon as one supposes that God is committed to the success of one regime, God himself acts to rebuke the supposition. God is God, and we are men, and there is an impenetrable mystery at the heart of his governance of nations. Perhaps the best theological commentary on this aspect of the prophetic faith was given, not in a work of theology, but in Lincoln's Second Inaugural Address made near the conclusion of the Civil War and just over a month before his death:

> Neither party expected for the war the magnitude or the duration which it has already attained. . . . Each looked for an easier triumph, and a result less fundamental and astounding. Both read the same Bible, and pray to the same God; and each invokes His aid against the other. . . . The prayers of both could not be answered—that of neither has been answered fully.
>
> The Almighty has His own purposes. . . .

The insight and the humility of these words capture the reverent Perhaps of the Old Testament faith.

C. H. Dodd has observed that in the Old Testament, the principle that governments are of divine institution is characteristically used "by way of menace to those who use their authority badly." [13] He cites the Wisdom of Solomon 6:1–5:

> Listen therefore, O Kings, and understand;
>   learn, O judges of the ends of the earth.
> Give ear, you that rule over multitudes,
>   and boast of many nations.
> For your dominion was given you from the Lord,
>   and your sovereignty from the Most High,
> who will search out your works and
>   inquire into your plans.
> Because as servants of his kingdom
>   you did not rule rightly,
> nor keep the law,
> nor walk according to the purpose of God,
> he will come upon you terribly and swiftly,
> because severe judgment falls on those in high places.

An apparent Hebrew Yes is thus, in use, really at most a Perhaps.

Partisans have sought to claim Jesus for the cause of revolt or for the cause of doctrinaire pacifism. But certainly the thing to be remarked is the slenderness of the evidence to which either side can appeal. Even in the politically explosive situation of his time, "the problem of the state is mentioned in Jesus' message only on the margin." [14] The evidence is not only small in quantity; it is complex. Jesus seems, on the one hand, to have agreed with such extreme factions as the Zealots that the existing order was to be overthrown; he is reported to have had Zealots among his followers; he was feared by his opponents as a firebrand and a threat to the order of the community; he was accused at his trial of a pledge to destroy the Temple itself; and the inscription on his cross marked him an insurrectionist. Yet he refused to use the sword for his ends; his kingdom was not of this world, else would his servants fight. The account we have of his behavior in the week of his death is not the story of a clever revolutionary. He made a dramatic (albeit peaceful) entry into Jerusalem and expelled those who bought and sold in the Temple; then he retreated to Bethany,

making daily forays into the city with a small, harmless band
of politically insignificant followers. He was betrayed by one
of his own associates and soon deserted by the rest. Officialdom
and public opinion, acting together, were able to have him put
away with little fear of uprising or clamor. As a political organ-
izer and activist, Jesus was notably unsuccessful. But he lacked
the awed deference to law, status, and rulers that mark the unquestioning supporter of the establishment.

Sherman Johnson comments, "One looks in vain in Jesus'
teaching for a clear indication of actual loyalty to any government. Civil obedience, yes; but not positive allegiance." [15] He
had the kind of inner dignity and authority that seemed to set
him above the law and above the worst the state could do. It
would seem that the New Testament Gospels do not want the
significance of Jesus to be interpreted primarily in any of the
available political roles. His kingdom and mission cut across
existing patterns of religion and government, but he did not
confront them by a direct challenge in force. Sherman Johnson
has summarized the matter:

> Although Jesus rejected the way of violence, which his com-
> patriots followed to their own destruction, he was actually crucified
> as a revolutionary. This is one of the great paradoxes of history.
> Perhaps the authorities feared him because they could not believe
> that a man with such a large popular following could have no
> political program. Jesus' avowed allegiance to the God of Israel,
> his detachment from Jewish and Roman leaders alike, did not
> fit into any conventional pattern. He was not even a pacifist holy
> man of the usual type. His opponents were baffled.[16]

The Perhaps of Jesus is obvious in his well-known reply to
the question about the lawfulness of paying tribute money. He
asked whose image was on the coin acceptable for the Roman
tax. He was told, "Caesar's." He confounded his questioners by
his pronouncement, "Render to Caesar the things that are
Caesar's and to God the things that are God's" (Mark 12:13–
17). This reply was not an evasion—even though it did avoid

the accusation of "traitor to Rome" or "Quisling of Rome" which a more direct answer might have gotten. Still less was his answer a decree concerning two swords or two coordinate realms between which all authority in human affairs was to be divided. He was saying something like: "The coin bears Caesar's image and can legitimately be used for his purposes, but men bear God's image and supremely belong to him." In irony, Jesus is drawing attention away from the question of imperial taxes and centering it on the ultimate relation and obligation of men to God.[17]

The presence of a Perhaps to the state in the New Testament epistles may be suggested by another reference to I Peter. The prominent theme of obedience to the state and to all human authority and of living honorably, peacefully, and blamelessly with one's neighbors has already been mentioned as a part of the New Testament Yes to the state. But this theme in I Peter is linked with another which qualifies it. This epistle emphasizes suffering and misunderstanding as things which fall to Christians, undeserved, as they fell to Christ—who endured them patiently. The counsel of I Peter, in this matter, seems to be: Obey the state and live blamelessly, but you can expect to suffer for it. Servants are urged to take patiently their unjustly inflicted suffering (2:18–25). All are encouraged in the midst of "suffering for righteousness' sake" (3:14–16), suffering "for doing right" (3:17), reproach and suffering "as a Christian" (4:12–16), and suffering "according to God's will" (4:19). Apparently at the time of the writing of I Peter the legal position of the church was such that to be a Christian at all put one in a position in which suffering at the hands of the state was a real possibility; in a sense, to profess Christian faith openly was already a kind of "civil disobedience." One might paraphrase: "The state is certain to be uncomprehending and likely to be brutal; but obey it anyway." Obedience here is not part of an unqualified Yes to the state; it is part of an agonized Perhaps.

The foregoing sketch will have indicated that the New

Testament evidence on the state is complex. Some of the Yes and the No statements are almost stark in their single-minded character. Some of the Perhaps passages reflect the many-sidedness of the question and the difficulty of Christian obedience. But the New Testament nowhere synthesizes these passages into a unified view of the state reconciling their apparent contradictions. The literature was produced out of a varied community living in varied conditions and written during several tumultuous decades of its early history. There was no occasion for a "nicely calculated less and more."

Thus, anyone who wishes to root his thought on civic duty in the New Testament must avail himself of the whole of the witness. Selectivity, in this matter, is irresponsible and certain to be misleading. Anyone who claims that "the New Testament as a whole is clearly against civil disobedience" has failed to reckon with the force of the biblical No. Anyone who would cite Jesus as "the archetype of lawbreakers" has not taken adequate account of the Yes.

Neither the Yes nor the No is declared in the Bible primarily on grounds of political theory. St. Paul does observe that the powers that be are a restraint on evil works, but this consideration is subordinate. Supremely both the Yes and the No are affirmed on the highest possible religious grounds. On the one hand, the powers that be are ordained by God; to resist them resists what he has appointed; a Christian is to be subject to human institutions *for the Lord's sake.* On the other hand, in disobeying men one acts out of personal obedience to God, who *must* be obeyed even when defiance of authority is entailed; when one suffers innocently, he is suffering as Christ also suffered and is entitled to "rejoice" and "glorify God" in the midst of persecution. Both the Yes and the No grow out of the relation to God. God has ordained government and given it a providential place in the establishment of order and the restraint of evil. Out of honor for God and his work, one should respect the powers that be. But the place given to human authority is corrupted; the state is at enmity with God; it is, before God, in the wrong, the very contradiction of his purposes. Hence there is a godly detachment from the demands of the rulers of this age; the new age has dawned, and human systems are under judgment.

This, in sum, is the ambivalence of the New Testament witness concerning the state—an ambivalence which has been echoed often in history when the church has been alert to the duality of its citizenship and the difficulty of its calling.[18] Any adequate use of the biblical material must reflect this ambivalence and its theological affirmation that God both establishes and judges our structures of authority.

three

: :

THE TRADITION
OF CHRISTIAN DISSENT (1)

The biblical No to the state (identified in the previous chapter) has continued over succeeding generations to inform a heroic tradition in which, when conditions have required, Christians have taught and practiced open defiance of authorities. (The Yes and the Perhaps, and mixtures among all three, have been perpetuated as well, of course.) It is obvious that this heritage of godly dissent is not widely known. When Christian civil disobedience is discussed nowadays, it is not uncommon to hear persons otherwise well informed speak as though it were a new issue. In their awareness of things, it is now coming up for the first time—or at best they think of disobedience as having been the counsel and practice of a few eccentrics. In this and the chapter following we shall call attention to some high points of this tradition. Even though this presentation of the issues must be brief, enough can be said to make it clear that the position of the present-day church is not without precedent for dissent from and disobedience to the state where it seems to be required out of obedience to God.

PRE-CHRISTIAN DISSENT: GREEK AND HEBREW

The claim of the individual conscience against the claim of the state is one of the oldest of human issues. It emerges as political thought emerges. Sophocles' *Antigone* contains one of the earliest instances of the theme—and still one of the most elo-

39

quent. Antigone has given token burial to the body of her slain
brother, Polynices, against the explicit orders of Creon, the
king. Her act is discovered, and she is brought before Creon.
She pleads that her act was one of piety in obedience to eternal,
unwritten laws—a claim which transcends any human ruler's
laws:

> Nor did I think your orders were so strong
> that you, a mortal man, could over-run
> the gods' unwritten and unfailing laws.
> Not now, nor yesterday's, they always live,
> and no one knows their origin in time.
> So not through fear of any man's proud spirit
> would I be likely to neglect these laws,
> draw on myself the gods' sure punishment. . . .
> But if I left that corpse, my mother's son,
> dead and unburied I'd have cause to grieve
> as now I grieve not.
> And if you think my acts are foolishness
> the foolishness may be in a fool's eye.[1]

Creon regards these words as insolent; he pleads the necessity
of authority and established order. Antigone's mind is of a
fundamentally different cast; she replies, "Nothing that you
say fits with my thought. I pray it never will." The rest of the
city, Creon states, has conformed to his regulation. Antigone
says that others approve her act but fear to speak. Creon asks,
"And you are not ashamed to think alone?" She is not. The
conflict marches to its tragic conclusion in the destruction both
of Antigone and of all that Creon holds dear. Remarkably
little has been added to the essentials of the issue since it was
movingly set forth in the sixth century B.C.

But conscientious disobedience to collective authority was
not, in Greek culture, only a matter of art. In an incident which
has captured the imagination of the West as have few others,
Athens, in 399 B.C., arrested and brought to trial Socrates—
its greatest philosopher, and perhaps its greatest son. Socrates

was accused of teaching impiety and, by his philosophizing, of corrupting the youth of Athens. The council, after hearing the case, found against Socrates, but it offered him his freedom if he would cease his practice of philosophy. Socrates replied:

> Many thanks indeed for your kindness, gentlemen, but I will obey the god rather than you, and as long as I have breath in me, and remain able to do it, I will never cease being a philosopher, and exhorting you, and showing what is in me to any one of you I may meet, by speaking to him in my usual way. . . . For this is what God commands me, make no mistake, and I think there is no greater good for you in the city in any way than my service to God. . . . Either let me go free or do not let me go free; but I will never do anything else, even if I am to die many deaths.[2]

Thus, in words hauntingly similar to those that were used four centuries later by the apostles, Socrates denied the right of a government to compel him to do something he could not with integrity do. The call to be a philosopher had not come from the state; if the state sought to forbid his following of it, Socrates could not comply. The result of the trial was that Socrates was put to death. Both the inability of governments to recognize true loyalty and the ability of an individual to affirm nobility of character through formal disobedience have a long history.

The Hebrews can hardly be said to have had a tradition of political thought. But their sense of being an elect community provided many themes which had importance for later political speculation and action. The Hebrew people were convinced that they were called in their father Abraham. The covenant between God and his people was renewed and explicated under Moses and the law. A brief period of splendor under David and Solomon validated the covenant. But, with the decline of the nation, the same word of God which had brought order out of primal chaos, which had called the fathers, given the law, and established the nation might be declared by the prophets against the nation. The God whose word was sent was Lord over all nations; his prophets, as servants of that word, were set

> over nations and over kingdoms,
> to pluck up and to break down,
> to destroy and to overthrow,
> to build and to plant.

Jeremiah 1:10

Thus the Jewish tradition had a strong sense of the creative purpose of God at work in the affairs of nations but also an awareness of the transcendence of that purpose over any particular nation—even their own. By the end of the prophetic period, the Jewish experience had witnessed men drawn by their apprehension of the word of God into open conflict with kings and popular opinion. They were "troublers of Israel," prepared when necessary to declare (at whatever cost to themselves) God's own No to the nation and its rulers.

When some of the Jews returned to their homeland after a brief captivity, they constituted only a weak nation subject to domination and often cruel persecution by greater powers. In this situation, Jewish confidence in the faithfulness of God and the fulfillment of his pledge had to live with sharp disappointment, and Jewish allegiance to God had to be tested and maintained against hostile powers. Various forms of compromise emerged, but so did heroism and inspired courage. During one persecution under the Selucid king Antiochus Epiphanes (who reigned from 175 to 163 B.C.), an unknown scribe wrote the book we know as Daniel. It contains two kinds of literature: incidents which are said to have befallen Daniel and his three friends in captivity in Babylon, and visions and interpretations concerning world history. The point of both is the same: devout Jews should show courage against the persecutor and not compromise their observance of the law, for those who trust in the living God are in the care of a Lord greater than nations and empires and have nothing finally to fear. Generations of Jews,

fighting gamely against a foreign occupying force and seeking
to uphold the purity of the law against paganizing forces, must
have taken courage from such passages as "Our God whom we
serve is able to deliver us from the burning fiery furnace; and
he will deliver us out of your hand, O King. But if not, be it
known to you, O King, that we will not serve your gods or
worship the golden image which you have set up." [3]

The two centuries from the book of Daniel to the destruction of the Temple in A.D. 70 were, for the Jewish people,
a period of intermittent but sometimes intense oppression. The
themes of suffering inflicted on the innocent and endurance
under persecution and martyrdom came to have an important
place in the theology and piety of Judaism.[4] The books of
I and II Maccabees, the whole of the apocalyptic literature, and
much of the distinctive writing from the Qumran community
illuminate the response of the Jewish community to these times
of testing. It is worth recalling that in the New Testament book
of Hebrews, the writer, a Christian, cites for the inspiration of
other Christians a list of Jewish persons of faith: "Some were
tortured, refusing to accept release, . . . Others suffered mock-
ing and scourging, and even chains and imprisonment. They
were stoned, they were sawn in two, they were killed with the
sword; . . . of whom the world was not worthy" (Hebrews
11:35–38).

THE PRIMITIVE CHURCH'S "NO"

To move to the Christian community, at the heart of the "rule of
faith" in which the primitive church confessed its faith in One
who is Lord of all and will be final judge of all, the church
set the phrase "Suffered under Pontius Pilate"—a reminder
that he had suffered at the order of the Roman state. The early
church, following its Lord, had, before it was a century old,
extensive experience of persecution and martyrdom. The attitude with which such oppression was met is suggested in a
somewhat cryptic passage from Revelation (13:10):

> If any one is to be taken captive,
>   to captivity he goes;
>
> if any one slays with the sword,
>   with the sword he must be slain.

The lines seem to be

. . . a warning against any attempt on the part of the Church to resist its persecutors. If a Christian is condemned to exile, . . . he is to regard exile as his allotted portion, and to go readily; if he is sentenced to death, he is not to lift his hand against the tyrant: to do so will be to deserve his punishment.[5]

Indeed, such an attitude marked the church throughout the first three centuries. There was no possibility of changing imperial policy. Neither representative processes nor constructive political discussion among common citizens existed. Actions and policies were made by a few powerful persons in Rome; there was no popular participation in government. Outright rebellion had been tried by some Jewish groups, and it was invariably self-defeating. Moreover, open revolt seemed not to have been the way chosen by Jesus. Imperial hostility could not be changed; it had to be endured. Indeed, the very idea that the conditions of political life might change and that some kind of social progress might lift the burden of oppression was unthinkable. The ideas of progress and social change had yet to be born. Civic protest in the ancient world (or for that matter until very recent generations) had to be undertaken without that support. So the early Christians praised the unyielding, steadfast, but gentle and Christlike way of meeting inevitable persecution.

But what was the cause of the official hostility? The earliest document in which an anti-Christian policy is explained is Pliny's well-known "Letter to Trajan" written from Bithynia about A.D. 112:

This is the course I have taken with those who are accused before me as Christians. I asked them whether they were Christians, and if they confessed, I asked them a second and a third time with threats of punishment. If they kept to it, I ordered them for execution; for I held no question that whatever it was that they admitted, in any case obstinacy and unbending perversity deserve to be punished. There were others of the like insanity; but these were Roman citizens, I noted them down to be sent to Rome.[6]

Some of the accused claimed not to have been Christians. They said a prayer to the gods (as all sensible persons would); they offered incense and wine to a statue of the emperor; and they cursed Christ. These persons were released. Pliny added a slight account of this superstition and the customs of its adherents as he understood them. Trajan replied, commending Pliny's handling of the matter.

Commenting on the policy expressed in this correspondence, Robert M. Grant writes:

The letters are a credit to the enlightened Roman administrative officials of the second century. Pliny obviously regards Roman religion as closely related to the life of the Roman state; he cannot understand those who are unwilling to use religious forms in attesting their loyalty to the state; all he asks for is compromise. He sees willingness to compromise among some who call themselves Christians, and he is therefore determined to break the spirit of civil disobedience. . . . The emperor shares his attitudes. The health and security of society is the most important matter.[7]

Thus the issue appeared to the officials of the empire to be civic in nature; one performed religious rites as gestures of patriotism or loyalty. Any superstition which produced obstinacy of the sort that some Christians demonstrated could be seditious in its tendencies.

The Christians, for their part, saw things quite otherwise. For them, Christianity was not one of the lightly held and lightly abandoned cults of the Hellenistic world. Being a Christian was a loyalty to Christ so complete that to curse one's Lord and perform an act of worship to the emperor was unthinkable.

One of the most moving testimonies to the sole Lordship of Christ was from an aged Christian, Polycarp, Bishop of Smyrna, who suffered martyrdom in A.D. 156. The officer who arrested this venerable man tried to persuade him: "Why, what harm is there in saying 'Caesar is Lord,' and burning the incense, and so on, and saving yourself?" But Polycarp remained unyielding. He was brought to the arena where the crowd called, "Kill the atheists." The governor tried once again to dissuade Polycarp, urging, "Take the oath, and I will let you go; revile Christ," to which Polycarp replied, "For eighty-six years I have been his slave, and he has done me no wrong; how can I blaspheme my king who has saved me?" Moments later he was burned.[8]

Far from being made disloyal citizens by their unshakable Christian allegiance, the early Christians protested that they were decent, honorable members of the community and that, in fact, their faith encouraged them in the duties of responsible, quiet, honest life. An early document pleads:

> Christians are not distinguished from the rest of mankind in country or speech or customs. . . . Like everyone else they marry, they have children, but they do not expose their infants. They set a common table, but not a common bed. They find themselves in the flesh, but they do not live after the flesh. They remain on earth, but they are citizens of heaven. They obey the established laws. They love all men, and are persecuted by all men.[9]

Such pleas reflect a time when, in the eyes and by the laws of the empire, to be a Christian at all was to be in a state of civil disobedience.

PROTEST AND EXPLANATION BY EARLY FATHERS

Further decrees outlawing Christian faith were made and enforced with varying energy throughout the period until Constantine. During this time, although the Christians could do little about their position except to suffer bravely, they did seek to explain and defend themselves in writing. Apologists and spokesmen pointed with humility and confidence to the witness of their fellow believers—their exemplary conduct and their serenity under torture. One such writer, the fiery North African, Tertullian, took issue with the laws under which Christians were held in their extra-legal status and made objects of persecution. (He had himself been a lawyer, and his experience of the profession seems to have removed any awe before law and lawmaking processes.) He wrote:

> I shall first discuss with you the question of the law, inasmuch as you are its protectors. In the first place, then, when you harshly lay down the law and say: "Your existence is illegal!" and when you make this charge without any further investigation—which would certainly be more humane—you make profession of violence and of an unjust, tyrannical domination, if you are saying that Christianity is illegal simply because that is your will, not because it really ought to be illegal. . . . If a law of yours has erred, it is, I presume, because it was conceived by man; it certainly did not fall from heaven.[10]

Tertullian continues his argument, pointing out that laws are in constant need of revision. The length of years it has been in effect and the worth of its founder do not constitute evidence enough to support a law which is unjust. He requests that the misdeeds alleged against Christians be investigated in each case and be proved or disproved. Condemnation on the basis of Christian profession alone he sees as grievously unjust.

Tertullian's contemporary, Origen, represented a basically different style of Christian mind. Yet these two giants of third-century Christian thought agreed that some civil laws can be unworthy of respect or obedience. In his great polemic *Contra Celsum* (written *ca.* A.D. 246–248), Origen takes up an argument of Celsus' that each nation's laws are right and binding for its citizens; whatever, in a given society, is traditional and approved is to be followed. Origen replies on the basis of the Stoic doctrine of natural law. He asks that a distinction among laws be recognized:

Now there are two kinds of law for our consideration. The one is the ultimate law of nature, which is probably derived from God, and the other the written code of cities. . . . Where the law of nature, that is of God, enjoins precepts contradictory to the written laws, consider whether reason does not compel a man to dismiss the written code and the intention of the lawgivers from his mind, and to devote himself to the divine Lawgiver and to choose to live according to His word, even if in doing this he must endure dangers and countless troubles and deaths and shame.[11]

Origen insists that there are "laws that are not laws," and these are not morally binding.

During this early period, the Christians had no social theory. They felt little stake in the society. Idolatry had so permeated many institutions of government and culture that Christians could not, in good conscience, practice certain professions important to the society. They lived, rather, on the margin of things. Moreover, the Christians expected that Christ would return at any moment and that this present order would be done away. They felt a godly detachment from the world's self-important systems which were destined not to endure. Yet they prayed for those in authority; they practiced the virtues of good neighbors and citizens; and they supported one another in the suffering which fell to them for the Name.

Ambrose and Augustine: Conflict and Criticism

With the Edict of Milan in A.D. 313, Christianity became a licit religion, and within a few years the emperor himself had become its convert and protector. Under Constantine the church and the clergy were increasingly granted corporate privileges; Christian institutions were legally observed; and rival pagan religions were proscribed.

From this time onward, the church began to have a responsible role in the social order. The world-renouncing attitudes of the previous era were carried over into the new in rigorous asceticism. The much-admired desert monks may have been the moral equivalent of the martyrs, but Christian leaders became persons of community status. Christian theology and ethics began to inform the ideas and institutions of the society. In short, for the next thousand years the civilization was engaged in the effort to articulate the meaning of Christian commonwealth.

These new directions are easy to identify, but progress met opposition, and the goal proved elusive.

A celebrated early instance of the tension between church and state is that involving St. Ambrose and his rebuke of two emperors. In A.D. 385, Valentinian (apparently at his mother's instigation) took steps to appropriate one of the churches of Milan for the use of the heretical Arian sect. Ambrose protested vigorously, and after a dramatic confrontation in which he seems to have had the support of the people he prevailed. Throughout this tension-filled episode, Ambrose showed great determination to maintain the claims of the church, a deep horror of violence and bloodshed, a personal dignity and a respectful manner in dealing with the emperor, and a repeatedly expressed willingness to let any pain and cost in the matter fall on himself. He wrote to his sister: "Indeed, I have arms, but only in the name of Christ. I have the power to offer my own body. . . . We have our own power. The priest's power is his weakness. 'When I am weak, then am I strong.' " [12] Of Ambrose's tactics at this point one writer has commented, "Passive resistance, here for the first time exercised in the grand style, will remain henceforth the most important weapon of the church in all controversies with the secular power." [13]

A second incident from Ambrose's life is better known. In A.D. 390, the emperor Theodosius, acting on an impulse which he quickly regretted but could not countermand in time, had seven thousand of the citizens of Thessalonica massacred as punishment for a riot. Ambrose was aghast but wrote a dignified letter to Theodosius, a member of his congregation, saying that he dared not offer the Sacrifice if the emperor intended to be present. This threat of excommunication was sufficient. Theodosius, to his great credit, made public penance.

Canon Greenslade urges that these better-known instances of ecclesiastical rebuke of the civil authorities not be regarded as isolated:

> Basil of Caesarea defied Valens, Martin of Tours challenged Maximus, Chrysostom vituperated the court of Constantinople, and Hosius of Cordova, once Constantine's confidential adviser, wrote thus to his successor Constantius: "Intrude not yourself into ecclesiastical matters, neither give commands unto us concerning them, but learn them from us. God hath put into your hands the kingdom: to us He hath entrusted the affairs of His Church; and, as he who should steal the empire from you would resist the ordinance of God, so likewise fear on your part lest, by taking upon yourself the government of the Church, you become guilty of a great offence." And not Athanasius alone, but a great company of bishops preferred exile to imperial perversions of the faith.[14]

Christian participation in and criticism of the political order were further advanced by Ambrose's great convert and pupil, Augustine. Even though much that Augustine wrote deals with the relation between Christian faith and the culture and history of the Roman world, Augustine seems not to have argued specifically the matter of civil disobedience. In fact, at one point in his episcopate, he used the power of civil government to repress a schismatic group—a precedent which was widely cited and followed for centuries and is now even more widely deplored.

But it should not be concluded from Augustine's failure to discuss civil disobedience or from his resort to civil authority for ecclesiastical purposes that he thought of government in an uncritical, positive way. In his most influential book, *The City of God,* he developed a sweeping view of history seen as a conflict between two cities organized around two loves: the city of God ordered by the love of God and the city of man moved by love of self. Augustine does not establish a direct identity between the city of God and the church or between the city of man and the state. Indeed, in *The City of God* he shows little interest in the institutional church. The reality of history is the mingling of these two cities and loves. Each is identified by its spirit and its destiny—Augustine's thought in the matter is eschatological. Neither "city" can be represented by a specific institution or community. His thinking is subtle. He takes issue with Cicero, who had argued that the state (specifically the Roman republic) was an embodiment of justice. Augustine asks, if justice is giving everyone his due, how any community which fails to yield God his proper honor can rightly be ordered according to justice (*Civ. Dei* XIX, 21). For Augustine, all states must, in this regard, be gravely defective. He did not, on this account, belittle the achievements of the Roman state—indeed, he praised them; the spirit of Rome was a stirring and precious thing to Augustine. But he considered that these achievements were, from one point of view, vices as long as there was no reference of life to the true God (XIX, 25). Augustine rejects Cicero's definition of the state in terms of justice and substitutes his own conception of human community as "an assemblage of reasonable beings bound together by a common agreement as to the objects of their love" (XIX, 24). This is a more empirical conception. He is able to look at communities as capable of great achievement but also as capable of great evil according to the direction of their loves. Indeed, kingdoms could be so unprincipled and rapacious as to be rightly regarded as "great robberies" (IV, 4).

This line of argument established for Augustine an independent Christian basis for criticism of the state. Government might be "ordained of God," but one need not for that reason stand in awe of it or suppose its actions to be irreproachable. Government originated in human sin. It was moved by pragmatic self-interest. Augustine thus maintained a detached, realistic—almost cynical—attitude toward the conduct of political units.

The later Christian tradition was able to conclude from portions of Augustine's ideas the theocratic notion that no state is complete unless it is explicitly Christian. But Augustine himself was too aware of the ambiguities of the political order and the impossibility of realizing the city of God in history to have stated this proposition himself in so simple a form.

MEDIEVAL TEACHERS ON DISOBEDIENCE

The following centuries in Europe were marked by the struggles of forces within a general unity provided by Christian belief. Ambrose had written, "Palaces belong to the emperor, churches to the bishop." [15] A duality was recognized. Spiritual matters contributing to eternal life were the sphere of the church and were in charge of its clergy. Temporal matters concerning the maintenance of order and justice were the business of the civil government and were in charge of its officials. These two authorities represented functions within a unified social order. Those who were civil authorities were at the same time Christian laymen and subject to spiritual discipline. The bishops, abbots, monks, and priests were also citizens, and they and their communities held political power and owed political loyalties. Under powerful personalities and historic forces, the prevailing definition of who received authority from whom would be questioned and altered. But in the clashes between the hierarchy and the empire, claims for the "church" against the "state" (as we now use the terms) were not made. By the high Middle Ages, the church was understood to be the whole of Christendom "of which the Papacy and the Empire were but the two executive arms." Any quarrel between the two "was considered not as a struggle between two independent institutions but as a schism in the Church." [16] In this situation, the task of the Christian political thinker was not to defend the beleaguered church against a hostile state but, rather, to formulate for the whole society a sense of ordered mutual relations in which the proper claims of ruler and ruled were alike taken into acount. If there were divine rights of kings (as all Christians agreed there were), there were also divine obligations. If subjects owed duties to rulers, they also could claim rights against rulers.

One of the notable political thinkers produced in the twelfth-century revival of learning was John of Salisbury. His large treatise, *Policraticus,* written in 1159, gathered up traditional Christian political wisdom; John was not an innovator. Throughout his work, he emphasizes the rule of law: "Between a tyrant and a prince there is this single or chief difference, that the latter obeys the law and rules the people by its dictates, accounting himself as but their servant." [17] Kings are not to rule according to their will and pleasure, but they are bound by those universal and perpetual laws which all nations must observe. Each of the words of the divine law "is thunder in the ears of princes." [18]

Most of this treatise is concerned with the prince and the character of his rule. But toward the end of the work, the author returns to the tyrant. The tyrant is head of a false state whose soul is a false church. The tyrant has overthrown the laws—laws which John has already shown to be the bond of the state. This constitutes the supreme treason and may be avenged by any citizen; the tyrant may be slain. Tyrannicide may have been only a theoretical possibility in the mind of so prudent and wise a man as John of Salisbury.[19] But it was a point required by his firm belief in a rule of law.

By the time of Thomas Aquinas, Aristotle's *Politics* had been rediscovered, and under that influence political thought took on greater complexity and rigor. Law, for Thomas, is not merely a matter of social regulation. All sovereignty in heaven and earth is from God. Law is the means of his rule. But Thomas distinguishes four kinds of law: eternal law, the law of God's own being and action; natural moral law, the objective moral order given in the nature of things; positive divine law, the revealed will of God for his creatures; and positive human law, rule promulgated for the human community by proper authority. Only the last of these categories refers to laws made by human agents. But human law, insofar as it corresponds with natural law, is a participation in the divine government of the world. Hence, to disobey such law is a fundamental rebellion against the moral order. But Thomas recognizes that positive human law does not always correspond with natural law, and it may be written in violation of divine law. Laws which are unjust "are acts of violence rather than laws; . . . they do not bind in conscience unless observance of them is required in order to avoid scandal or public disturbance." [20] And law contravening the divine law "ought not to be obeyed." [21] Moreover, a ruler has a trust to fulfill. If he abuses his position and governs unjustly, he need not be obeyed: "Man is bound to obey secular rulers to the extent that the order of justice requires. For this reason if such rulers have no just title to power, but have usurped it, or if they command things to be done which are unjust, their subjects are not obliged to obey them." [22] Indeed, Aquinas maintains that tyrants can be deposed (though, unlike John of Salisbury, he recommends their permanent rustication rather than outright tyrannicide).

The neat, well-ordered system of St. Thomas probably, even in its own time, represented a theoretical formulation rather than a description of a happy accord among the power centers of the late Middle Ages. Certainly the following centuries are marked by a variety of the strongest absolutisms, all championed or opposed by partisans of a different temper from that of Scholastic synthesis. As the claims for papal sovereignty were extended, they were vigorously opposed by Marsilia of Padua and William of Occam. William regarded extreme papal claims as a heresy, and he maintained the rights against the papacy of the whole body of Christian believers. "The theory of papal *plenitudo potestatio* was the first definite claim in the Middle Ages to a power that was absolute, indefeasible, and sovereign." [23] It was countered in the name of a liberated faith, not in the name of rationalism. The two opposing forces were both within the church, and both argued on essentially medieval Christian grounds. There was a widespread wish for papal absolutism to be moderated by the call of a church council. William of Occam, for his part, was quite clear that such a council might err—but, if it were fully representative (including laity and specifically women), it would be less likely to err than would the unchecked opinions of the papacy.

In the next century, John Wycliffe opposed the same papal absolutism by an appeal to the monarchy. Indeed, his deference to royal authority came very close to unlimited obedience, but he resorted to paradox. In a characteristic doctrine, he held that a tyrant had power but not Lordship. Wycliffe commends passive obedience even to such a king. But he argues that one can obey by resisting. He goes on "to inculcate the duty of rebellion and even tyrannicide as possible modes of obedience." [24] With obedient citizens of that mind, a ruler would seem to have no need for revolutionaries.

During the centuries covered in this chapter, the Christian No took two forms. In the era of persecution, it was declared in action by martyrdom and faithfulness unto death. In the era of Christendom, it was declared by teachers who recognized that rulers might betray their God-given trust and that in such circumstances citizens had a God-given right to disobey.

four

: :

THE TRADITION
OF CHRISTIAN DISSENT (2)

As it entered the modern era, the church had to find ways of obedience under new conditions. By the sixteenth century, nations governed by absolute monarchs had become the common form of political community. Undoubtedly princes had acted on utterly pragmatic motives before Niccolò Machiavelli advised them on theory and strategy. But at the Renaissance the force of royal absolutism was newly in the open, and Christians had to reckon with it. Under this challenge, the Christian response took various forms. The Christian No was restated by great leaders in various idioms. Some traditions came to such an accommodation with rulers that the No almost passed into complete eclipse. Elsewhere it was acted on with marked heroism, and a number of the cherished freedoms of our modern world were in part secured by the practice of Godly dissent.

LUTHER AND LUTHERANISM

Martin Luther mounted a thoroughgoing revolution against the medieval church. Its structure, doctrines, piety, liturgy, and philosophy were all radically criticized. But in the same process, Luther adopted what seems now to be an unnecessarily uncritical alliance with the "Godly princes" who supported his cause. He went further and counseled that passive obedience was due even to evil rulers, "For even when the government commits an injustice . . . God wants the government obeyed,

56

without treachery or deception." [1] Luther recognized the disparity between his revolt against ecclesiastical authority and his acceptance of civil maladministration. He defended himself by observing that spiritual authority is so important a matter that its errors should be opposed vigorously, but civil authority is so relatively minor a matter that its failings should be borne in patience.[2]

Luther developed a distinctive doctrine of the "two kingdoms." The church and the state are separate realms. God is Lord of both, and Christians are members of both. The church is to have the freedom to do its distinct spiritual work. The state, for its part, has its own integrity. It derives no authority from the church. It should serve its own purposes free of church interference.

The result of this emphasis is that the Lutheran tradition has been inclined to passivity in the face of the state. Lutheran churches have been reluctant to criticize the social and political order. An attitude of submissiveness and quietism toward worldly powers has characterized the tradition. Luther frequently expressed his opinion that resistance to civil authority is in all circumstances morally wrong. "Disobedience is a sin worse than murder, unchastity, theft, dishonesty, and all that goes with them." [3]

But Luther's opinions were responsive to changing circumstances.[4] He never seriously worked for systematic consistency in his ideas. He tended to express himself emphatically and without qualification on whichever side of an issue he was speaking. In the very treatise, *Of Good Works,* from which all of our earlier direct quotations from Luther have been taken, he states the complement to the doctrine for which he is best known:

But if, as often happens, the temporal power and authorities, or whatever they call themselves, would compel a subject to do something contrary to command of God, or hinder him from doing what God commands, obedience ends and the obligation ceases.

In such a case a man has to say what St. Peter said to the rulers of the Jews, "We must obey God rather than men." [5]

This emphasis is less frequently and less fully stated in Luther, but it is present, and the Lutheran tradition has not forgotten it.[6]

CALVIN AND CALVINISM

John Calvin shared Luther's horror of anarchy and, like Luther, he stressed a passive obedience to civil authority. Government is of God's establishment. Magistrates, he taught, "are invested with his authority, are altogether his presentatives, and act as his viceregents." [7] Calvin's view of the state, however, was not inclined toward a "two swords" division of spheres. [Calvin stressed the unity of church and government as distinguishable functions under the sovereign rule of God. This emphasis looked in a theocratic direction.] The state was to be so ordered as to help make Christians. But in Calvin's theory, the church was not to rule the state; the church served a higher function than the state "because it was the guardian of the Word of God from which all authority in Church and State derived." [8]

The duty of the state was to support the rites and doctrines of the church and to provide for general peace and justice. Calvin took account of the possible failure of government to serve these purposes. Should government betray the intentions for which it is ordained, it might justly be resisted. But Calvin assigned the responsibility for this resistance to "lesser magistrates" rather than to private citizens.[9]

Thus, for Calvin, government was limited by its own assigned functions. Resistance was allowed for when government overstepped its ordained role. But in a situation in which the government was sympathetic to a Calvinist regime or where a regiment of saints prevailed, this doctrine worked in a conservative fashion. When, however, the government was hostile, "it required no fundamental modification of Calvin's theory to make it extremely revolutionary." [10] The Calvinist theory of resistance was not brought into play by Calvin at Geneva where he had things largely his own way. But the Calvinist tradition drew inspiration from it for radical resistance in such places as France, Scotland, Holland, and England where the governments were not in sympathy with Reformed principles. In such circumstances, the Calvinist emphasis on the church's supreme duty to God was asserted—asserted against the majesty of the state and with great personal cost, if necessary. John Knox's trumpet blasts are well enough known. After the terrible St. Bartholomew's Day Massacre, Beza was led, on Calvinist principles, to say more than Calvin himself had said against the authority of a state which would persecute Protestant citizens. From Huguenot sources there emerged in 1579 a work called *Vindiciae Contra Tyrannos,* which became "one of the landmarks of revolutionary literature." [11] The book bases government on a primal contract between God and a king, which contract works through a contract between king and people. The authority of the king is thus conditional. If the king violates the law of God, it becomes lawful for the people to resist him. Indeed, it becomes their duty. If they fail to resist, the guilt of the king's default is laid to the people. Grotius and Althusius in the Netherlands were Reformed theologians with similar insistence on the limitations of earthly rulers. Thus it will be evident that the tradition emerging from the clear, conservative work of John Calvin was capable of revolutionary development.

THE ENGLISH CHURCH AND THE MONARCHY

On the Continent, as we have noted, a case had been made by Protestant spokesmen for limited monarchy. In a parallel development, a tradition of Roman Catholic legal and political thinkers argued to the same effect. The Jesuit casuists Bellarmine, Moriana, and Suarez are perhaps the best-known representatives of this tradition. They seem to have argued for a limited monarchy so that kings would be less vigorous rivals to papal power. They held that revolt against schismatic monarchs was justifiable.[12] Thus Continental Protestants and papists agreed in defending limited monarchy and a Christian right to resist. Both sides linked religious and political arguments.

In England, this development across the Channel was regarded with suspicion; it was a case of Herod and Pilate becoming friends. Two distrusted forces seemed to have agreed in taking a wrong direction. The right of ecclesiastical institutions to restrict monarchs had been asserted by both Rome and Geneva. One writer (typical of many) said: "They are both inconsistent with monarchy and indeed with all government; over which they pretend a power and jurisdiction by Christ, the one for the Pope, the other for the Presbytery; from which there lies no appeal." [13] If these two forces were agreed that the king's power should be limited, the doctrine must be mistaken. It would have to be answered by a religious and political affirmation of absolute monarchy.

The earliest steps of the English Reformation had been taken by royal initiative. The independence of the Church of England from the papacy was a jurisdictional matter initially rather than a movement driven by powerful religious forces. By the time an intellectual formulation of the meaning of the reformed Christianity of England was possible, royal headship was already a reality.

The second collection of homilies, issued in 1562, contained "An Homily against Disobedience and Wilful Rebellion." The argument of this address roots civil obedience in a universal order and designates rebellion as "both the first and greatest and the very root of all other sins." [14] Since no prince's rule will ever be universally liked, if those subjects who wished for change were free to rebel, "no realm should ever be without rebellion." When "an undiscreet or evil prince" rules, it is a rebuke sent by God as punishment for sins, and rebellion against such a prince is rebellion against the wisdom of God.

The example of David is cited who, despite the manifest inadequacy of Saul, would not "lay hand upon the Lord's anointed." The sermon assembles all possible arguments on behalf of obedience and allows for no alternative. "Let us good subjects, I say, . . . avoid and flee all rebellion, as the greatest of all mischiefs."

Lest it sound as though Christian ethical sanctions were being used, in explosive times, as an instrument of Tudor policy without theological integrity, Richard Hooker requires a hearing. The massive polemic of Hooker was aimed principally at the Puritans, who sought to qualify their obedience to ecclesiastical ordinances until the church had corrected itself after the Genevan model. Hooker argued with great impressiveness that the Puritans were striking against the roots of all political order. His argument is close to St. Thomas in its depiction of law as the basis for cosmic order binding ruler and ruled. Like Thomas, he distinguishes types of law. But he nowhere discusses what should be done when positive human law violates the laws of nature and reason. He nowhere discusses tyranny and what might responsibly be done about it. He is so favorably disposed toward the English monarchy and ecclesiastical system and regards the objections of the Puritans as so arbitrary that he is not compelled to ask, "What if the existing system were not as benign as it is?"

But, even though Hooker does not consider civil disobedience,[15] his system is far from repressive or absolutist. His structuring of types of law at least introduces the conditional character of human regulations and the possibility of their being grievously in error by some ascertainable standard. Moreover, Hooker contended for a principle of consent. "Laws they are not which public approbation have not made so." [16] Government is established by a contract; to govern without consent is tyranny. He describes no way in which this consent once entered upon can be withdrawn. Yet the consent (usually given through one's representatives) is basic to the very nature of government. It is this conditional, limiting side of Hooker's thought which was most productive in the minds of Locke and other political philosophers who drew on the *Ecclesiastical Polity*. "What power the king hath he hath it by law, the bounds and limits of it are known." [17] Even though he allowed no place for conscientious disobedience and conceded no right of rebellion, his essentially conservative work took such adequate account of the complexity of human life that his influence in the history of thought has not been on the side of absolutism; he has been an emancipating influence.

In the Stuart period in England, the claim for the divine right of kings was advanced to extreme heights—and acquiesced in by ecclesiastics. Indeed, rebellion against the king became the supreme sin. The interests of the monarch and the interests of the church were identified. Presbyterian and Papist alike were putting forward claims to control the state for ecclesiastical advantage. The reply took the form of the church declaring itself subservient to the monarchy:

> The most high and sacred order of kings is of divine right, being the ordinance of God himself, founded in the prime laws of nature, and clearly established by express texts both of the Old and New Testaments. A supreme power is given to this most excellent order by God himself in the scriptures, which is, that kings should rule and command in their several dominions all persons of what rank or estate soever, whether ecclesiastical or civil, and that they should restrain and punish with the temporal sword all stubborn and wicked doers.
>
> The care of God's church is so committed to kings in the scripture, that they are commended when the church keeps the right way, and taxed when it runs amiss. . . .
>
> For any person to set up, maintain, or avow in any of their said realms or territories respectively, under any pretence whatsoever, any independent coactive power, either papal or popular, (whether directly or indirectly,) is to undermine their great royal office, and cunningly to overthrow that most sacred ordinance which God himself hath established; and so is treasonable against God as well as against the king.

For subjects to bear arms against their kings, offensive or defensive, upon any pretence whatsoever, is at least to resist the powers which are ordained of God; and though they do not invade, but only resist, St. Paul tells them plainly they shall receive to themselves damnation.[18]

The churchman's first line of defense against Puritanism and Popery seemed to be the king's prerogative. This prerogative was exercised under the law of God and of nature; the doctrine did not hold that the king could be irresponsible but, rather, that he had a higher degree of responsibility than the ordinary citizen. An evil king would be judged by God. But, as he was himself the origin and repository of lawful authority, the king could not be judged by his subjects.

This doctrine—represented in other nations beside England, of course—was a survival of part of the medieval tradition without other compensating doctrines. That it was out of touch with the forces of its time will be suggested by noting that the declaration quoted above was issued just two years before the English Civil War broke out and nine years before the king was executed. The divine right of kings was an episode (not altogether discreditable) in the transition to modern constitutional government without church control or participation. It is mentioned here as one of the outstanding moments during which civil disobedience was rejected categorically by a portion of the church.

Even among loyal Anglicans in the seventeenth century, however, other opinions flourished. The moral theologians held a balanced view of civic obligation. Jeremy Taylor's *Ductor Dubitantium* may be taken as a representative discussion. Taylor lays down a basic rule: "The conscience is properly and directly, actively and passively, under pains of sin and punishment, obliged to obey the laws of men." [19] This rule does not deny that "God only is Lord of consciences" or that "all Christians are free men." For human lawgivers are agents of God. This rule applies "regularly and ordinarily," but there are situations which introduce new considerations. If death or "an intolerable or very grievous evil" might result from obedience, the law is not binding. (God's law ought not to be broken even to save one's life, Taylor explains. But he is here speaking of mere human laws about things otherwise indifferent.) Further, "the laws of our superior that are not just and good do not oblige the conscience," for "To establish anything that is unjust or evil is against the nature of laws." To obey such a law were it to be set forth would compound the wrong. "A law is unjust if it is made by incompetent authority, if a competent authority exceeds the limits of his power in making it, if the law does not contribute to the public good, or if the burden it imposes is greater than the evil it seeks to remedy." [20] Taylor suggests some cautions to be observed before active disobedience is undertaken. These, in Thomas Wood's summary, are:

> Our disobedience must not be such that it will lead to scandal, or encourage men to rebel, or make religion and duty lightly regarded. Moreover, the public inconvenience arising from what is thought to be an unjust law must be *evident, certain,* and *notorious;* if there is any doubt, the presumption is always on the side of obedience to our lawful superior; and if the law seems unjust only to an individual he may petition for dispensation and equity, but otherwise must be prepared to bear private hardship for the public good.[21]

In addition, Taylor requires that a law must be given sufficient promulgation before it can be considered binding.

In this summary we can do little more than hint at the large body of seventeenth-century casuistical divinity in which (during an era of passion and division) the problem of civil disobedience was discussed thoroughly and with great wisdom.

THE SECTARIAN "NO"

There is another tradition that also requires mention. Alongside those who thought the government should be subservient to the church and those who thought the church should be subservient to the king, there was a group (represented on the Continent as well as in England) which proclaimed that the church received no authorization from the state and was not answerable to the state. It seemed to opponents at the time that these curious sectarians merely wanted their own styles of doctrine and organization so badly that they would break public peace to secure them—and, in the process, they promoted nonessentials to primary issues of conscience. It has seemed to later critics that by the appeal to individual conscience which recognized no sovereign but God, religion was made too private and individualistic a thing to have the engagement with public affairs that it ought to have. But to its defenders, this tradition seemed to have brought living Christian faith into its own. Religion was declared to be no affair of the state; faith, it was held, could not be compelled or forbidden by civil authority. Religious institutions own no Lord but God. They must be accorded freedom (within the requirements of public responsibility) to develop along lines of their own as voluntary associations. In the Elizabethan period, as this tradition was emerging, one of its earliest spokesmen, Robert Browne, wrote in his *Treatise of Reformation Without Tarrying for Anie:*

If either Magistrate or other would take that (liberty) from us, we must not give place by yielding unto them, no, not for an hour. And this liberty is the free use of our callings and gifts, as we see most agreeing to the worde of God, and expedient for his glorie. . . . And this dispensation did not the Magistrate give me, but God by the consent and ratifying of the Church, and therefore as the Magistrate gave it not, so can he not take it away. Indeed, if God take it away for my wickedness and evil desert, he may remove me from the Church, and withhold me from preaching. But if God do it not, and his worde doth approve me, as most meet for that calling, I am to preach still, except I be shut up in prison, or otherwise with violence withheld from my charge.[22]

These words announce a tradition of defiance to oppressors of conscience which was maintained until the actuality of religious pluralism began to be recognized in England.

An instance of this tradition in action is available in *A Relation of the Imprisonment of Mr. John Bunyan,* which tells of Bunyan's arrest and imprisonment at Bedford in 1660 for illegal preaching. The narrative is largely given through encounters between the prisoner and his judges and visitors. One visitor, Mr. Cobb, was sent by the court to urge Bunyan to submit to the Church of England. The conversation is reported to have gone:

Cobb. You know, saith he, that the Scripture saith, *the powers that are, are ordained of God.*
Bunyan. I said, yes, and that I was to submit to the King as supreme, also to the governors, as to them that are sent by him.
Cobb. Well then, said he, the King then commands you, that you should not have any private meetings; because it is against his law, and he is ordained of God, therefore you should not have any.
Bunyan. I told him that *Paul* did own the powers that were in his day, as to be of God; and yet he was often in prison under them for all that. And also, though *Jesus Christ* told *Pilate,* that he had no power against him, but of God, yet he died under the same *Pilate;* and yet, said I, I hope you will not say, that either *Paul,* or Christ, was such as did deny magistracy, and so sinned against God in slighting the ordinance. Sir, said I, the law hath provided two ways of obeying: The one to do that which I in my conscience do believe that I am bound to do, actively; and where I cannot obey actively, there I am willing to lie down, and to suffer what they shall do unto me. At this he sate still and said no more.[23]

This tradition is worth noting, for its affirmation of the sole dependence of the church on Christ is an insight from which most churches of the modern world have learned. Many of them have had to rediscover it when, in cataclysmic events, the cultural and governmental supports on which they had counted were withdrawn. Further, it was this Puritan and Separatist tradition which was brought to the New England colonies, whence it has exerted a powerful influence on the style and shape of religious institutions in America.

CIVIL DISOBEDIENCE IN AMERICAN SOCIETY

There has been a curious counterpoint in American life between, on the one hand, the legal-mindedness of the society and, on the other hand, the frequency with which portions of the community have acted apart from the established laws either to exempt themselves from onerous requirements, or to secure for themselves political recognition, or to alter the policies of government, or even to take justice into their own hands. Some of these actions taken apart from law seem in historical retrospect to have been narrowly self-assertive in motive and destructive in their accomplishments; any account attempting a moral or legal defense of such lawless actions is manifestly self-justifying. But the judgment of history has been kinder to other acts of open dissent. It is well to remember that such gains as the achievement of religious liberty, the elimination of slavery, the granting of the franchise to women, the recognition of the rights of organized labor, the acknowledgment in law of conscientious objection to military service, the securing of the civil rights of minority groups—not to speak of the very existence of the American nation itself—were all accomplished in part by acts which were at the time illegal. American society owes much to its disobedients. The account of this debt cannot be given within the limits of this chapter. The story of civil disobedience (even of religiously motivated disobedience) in America has not been adequately told. But it may be possible here to suggest some of the places where it is apparent at once that there is something to tell.

Though the founders of Massachusetts left England in part because there was no liberty there for church order and worship of the kind they sought, they did not establish religious liberty in the New World. The regime they established was authoritarian and repressive; civil disabilities were maintained against unregenerate persons; and those whose beliefs or practices differed from the Puritan norm were subject to persecution. The conscience for whose expression the Massachusetts authorities contended was their own. The general principle that a person's religious beliefs were no affair of the government was an unfamiliar idea, and it had to win (and indeed is still winning) its way slowly.

For preaching strange doctrines and raising unwelcome questions, Roger Williams was banished by the Massachusetts authorities into the "howling wilderness." He founded the colony of Rhode Island, which became a refuge of religious liberty. In 1644 he wrote his celebrated treatise *The Bloudy Tenent of Persecution,* in which he vigorously attacked persecution for cause of conscience and argued that religious belief could not be coerced. Four of Williams's theses suggest the mind of the man:

The blood of so many hundred thousand souls of Protestants and Papists, spilt in the Wars of present and former Ages, for their respective Consciences, is not required nor accepted by Jesus Christ the Prince of Peace.

All Civil States with their Officers of justice in their respective constitutions and administrations are proved essentially Civil, and therefore not Judges, Governors or Defenders of the Spiritual of Christian State and Worship.

It is the will and command of God, that (since the coming of his Son the Lord Jesus) a permission of the most Paganish, Jewish, Turkish or Antichristian consciences and worships, be granted to all men in all Nations and Countries: and they are only to be fought against with that Sword which is only (in Soul matters) able to conquer, to wit, the Sword of God's Spirit, the Word of God.

God requireth not an uniformity of Religion to be inacted and inforced in any civil state; which inforced uniformity (sooner or later) is the greatest occasion of civil War, ravishing of conscience, persecution of Christ Jesus in his servants, and of the hypocrisy and destruction of millions of souls.[24]

These characteristic ideas should not lead anyone to suppose that Williams was a liberal humanist born out of due time. His thinking was rigorously Puritan in presuppositions and manner. But in the matter of religious liberty, his ideas (which would be widely shared today by people who would not comprehend his way of arriving at them) showed an insight not frequently found in the early seventeenth century.

When Quaker missionaries arrived in New England in the 1650's, they were persecuted mercilessly. Laws in Massachusetts assigned penalties for bringing Quakers into the colony and heavy fines for the holding of Quaker meetings. In 1658 a further law imposed the death penalty on Quakers who might return after banishment from the colony. Under this law at least four persons were hanged by 1661. Others were beaten or branded or had their ears cropped. The cruel persecution in 1657 at Flushing, Long Island, of a young Quaker, Robert Hobson, by the government of New York led to some public revulsion against the anti-Quaker laws and the vigor with which they were administered. This feeling is represented by the "Flushing Remonstrance" drawn up by the men of the community. The document said in part:

Love, peace and libertie extending to all in Christ Jesus, Condemns hatred, warre and bondage; and because our Savior saith it is impossible but that offence will come, but woe be unto him by whom they commeth, our desire is not to offend one of his little ones in whatsoever forme, name or title hee appears in, whether Presbyterian, Independent, Baptist or Quaker; but shall be glad to see anything of God in any of them: desireing to doe unto all men as wee desire all men should doe unto us, which is the true law both of Church and State; . . . Therefore is any of these said persons come in love unto us, wee cannot in Conscience lay violent hands upon them, but give them free Egresse into our Towne and howses as God shall perswade our Consciences.[25]

Eventually, William Penn, a Quaker aristocrat, founded Pennsylvania not only as a settlement for Quakers but also as a "holy experiment" in religious freedom for those of all faiths or none.

The free exercise of religion, the breaking of a monopoly by any single religious group, the separation of all religious bodies from the state, the full participation in civic affairs of persons of all persuasions—gains of which Americans generally would be proud—were secured in part by persons who followed conscience in defiance of laws and authorities.

All through the colonial period the New England clergy had taught that: "As long as a king enforced God's commands, embodying them in human laws, the people owed him obedience and assistance. If, however, moved by his own depravity, he violated God's commands or failed to enforce them, he broke the compact on which his political authority rested, and it was the people's duty to remove him lest God visit the whole community with death and destruction." [26] But this doctrine had not had a revolutionary sound. It was standard Calvinist political theory taught by an authoritarian church in a community governed by saints. The only king to which it might apply was an ocean away. But rather rapidly in the generation prior to 1775 the revolutionary implications of these familiar ideas began to be articulated. The role of religion in the intellectual currents of the revolutionary period was complex. Certainly a fair number of the clergy (especially of the Church of England) were Tory in sympathy. Their cause lost, and they tend to be little-remembered if not discredited. But this group contained high-minded men who, by the standards of eighteenth-century divinity, may have been better Christians than were the preachers of rebellion. But a great many other clergy were wholehearted participants in the cause of independence. Clinton Rossiter has put it strikingly: "Had ministers been the only spokesmen of the American cause, and Jefferson, the Adamses, and Otis never appeared in print, the political thought of the Revolution would have followed almost exactly the same line—with perhaps a little more mention of God, but certainly no less of John Locke." [27] The relation between this revolutionary sympathy and Christian doctrine is unclear. Historians had generally maintained that preachers of revolution were to be found among the more liberal Christian spokesmen, who had been influenced by rationalist ideas. But the most recent and extensive reinvestigation of the evidence, Alan Heimert's great study, *Religion and the American Mind*,[28] finds that passionate commitment to the rights of men (and of Englishmen in particular) and opposition to oppression were strongest in the centers of vital orthodoxy; many of the rationalist clergy were politically indifferent. In any case, revolutionary ideas were supported by a wide group of thoughtful Christian leaders. One of the most often quoted of such spokesmen was Jonathan Mayhew, of West Church, Boston, who combined theological liberalism and political radicalism. In his celebrated sermon "A Discourse Concerning Unlimited Submission," he took occasion from the anniversary of the death of Charles I to argue at length on the conditional nature of Christian obedience, the nature of tyranny, and the right of resistance:

A people really oppressed in a great degree by their sovereign, cannot well be insensible when they are so oppressed. . . . For a nation thus abused to arise unanimously and resist their prince, even to the dethroning him, is not criminal, but a reasonable way of vindicating their liberties and just rights: it is making use of the means, and the only means, which God has put into their power for mutual and self defence. And it would be highly criminal in them not to make use of this means. It would be stupid tameness and unaccountable folly for whole nations to suffer *one* unreasonable, ambitious, and cruel man to wanton and riot in their misery. And in such a case, it would, of the two, be more rational to suppose that they that did not resist, than that they who did, would receive to themselves damnation.[29]

It might be urged that the arguments of the patriot pulpit sounded very like arguments of secular political theorists. Some sermons and political pamphlets would be all but indistinguishable. (Observe the appeal to "reasonableness" in the Mayhew passage above.) The intellectual ancestry of this preaching seems to have been Locke and Montesquieu; it shows little theological independence or any distinctive bond with the Christian message. But it might be equally well argued that the political ideas of the Enlightenment showed some dependence on Grotius, Hooker, or Milton. For over thirteen hundred years the political tradition and the theological tradition had interacted closely. Since the Christian gospel is not itself a political theory, the only ideas a Christian thinker has as material for the consideration of civic obligation are the political ideas current in his time. The Christian preachers of the revolutionary period were men of integrity; they considered the available political realities and theories in the light of the Christian faith as they understood it—no one can do more. And they confidently proclaimed that the overthrow of tyranny was a duty under God. The preacher Andrew Eliot said simply that when tyranny is abroad, "submission is a crime." [30]

Ethical issues continued in the forefront of American thought in the nineteenth century. There has been so much interest in the New England Transcendentalists as moral prophets that it is useful to have a new study, *Civil Disobedience and Moral Law in Nineteenth-Century American Philosophy,* by Edward H. Madden, which sets the Transcendentalists alongside another tradition termed "academic orthodoxy." The spokesmen of this less-well-known tradition tended to be explicitly Christian (touched by varying degrees of liberal influence) and respected educators. Their influence in American thought in the years before the Civil War was very great. Madden calls attention, as an example, to Francis Wayland, president of Brown University and author of widely used textbooks in moral philosophy. Wayland was outraged by the Mex-

ican War and delivered in 1847 three sermons on "The Duty
of Obedience to the Civil Magistrate." In them he argued for
civil disobedience in forceful terms:

The magistrate may not only do wrong himself, but he may
command me to do wrong. How shall I regard this command? I will
regard it as I do any other command to do wrong,—I will not
obey it. I will look the magistracy calmly and respectfully in
the face, and declare to it that in this matter I owe it no allegiance.
I will have nothing to do with its wrong-doing. I will separate
myself, as far as possible, from the acts and its consequences,
whether they be prosperous or adverse. It is wickedness; it has
the curse of God inwrought into it, and I will have nothing to do
with it. . . . The magistracy may punish me; I cannot help that.
I will not resist, but I will not do wrong, nor will I be a party
to wrong, let the magistracy or aught else command me.[31]

As for the Transcendentalists, their general view of man
as taught by intuition and oppressed and corrupted by institutions is well known. Thoreau's essay "Civil Disobedience" is
so widely reprinted that perhaps mere mention of it in this
place will be sufficient. His address "A Plea for Captain John
Brown" is less widely known and is an equally eloquent document. John Brown had been brought to Thoreau's home in
1857, and Thoreau had heard him speak. The news of Brown's
raid in 1859 moved Thoreau deeply, and he filled pages of his
journal with his thoughts. A few days later he delivered his
remarkable address—an event all but unnoticed at the time.
In this plea, Thoreau had moved from the attitude of passive
disaffiliation expressed in "Civil Disobedience" to entertain the
possibility that violence might be necessary in a good cause.

The politicians assert that the only proper way by which de-
liverance is to be obtained is by "the quiet diffusion of the sentiments
of humanity," without any "outbreak." As if the sentiments of
humanity were ever found unaccompanied by its deeds, and you
could disperse them, all finished to order, the pure article, as
easily as water with a watering-pot, and so lay the dust. . . .

"All is quiet at Harper's Ferry," say the journals. What is the character of that calm which follows when the law and the slaveholder prevail? I regard this event as a touchstone designed to bring out, with glaring distinctness, the character of this government. . . . When a government puts forth its strength on the side of injustice, as ours to maintain slavery and kill the liberators of the slave, it reveals itself a merely brute-force, or worse, a demoniacal force. It is the head of the Plug-Uglies. It is more manifest than ever that tyranny rules. . . .

It was his peculiar doctrine that a man has a perfect right to interfere by force with the slaveholder, in order to rescue the slave. I agree with him. They who are continually shocked by slavery have some right to be shocked by the violent death of the slaveholder, but no others. Such will be more shocked by his life than by his death. I shall not be forward to think him mistaken in his method who quickest succeeds to liberate the slave. I speak for the slave when I say that I prefer the philanthropy of Captain Brown to that philanthropy which neither shoots me nor liberates me. . . . I do not wish to kill nor to be killed, but I can foresee circumstances in which both these things would be by me unavoidable.[32]

This address was virtually Thoreau's last public utterance.

The same event moved another eloquent man to comment memorably on civil disobedience. The abolitionist movement had repeatedly declared its conviction that unjust laws might be broken. Indeed, some abolitionists had attacked the Constitution itself because it countenanced slavery. Moreover, the Fugitive Slave Law was understood to be a patently evil law; it was disobeyed; and its enforcement was hindered. Out of this background of questioning legal structures in the light of the self-evident evil of slavery, the abolitionists had a strong, articulated point of view. The orator and aristocrat Wendell Phillips delivered a notable address on John Brown in which he spoke of disobedience:

But John Brown violated the law. Yes. On yonder desk lie the inspired words of men who died violent deaths for breaking the laws of Rome. Why do you listen to them so reverently? Huss and Wickliffe violated laws; why honor them? George Washington, had he been caught before 1783, would have died on a gibbet, for breaking the laws of his sovereign. Yet I have heard that man praised within six months. Yes, you say, but these men broke *bad* laws. Just so. It is honorable, then, to break *bad* laws, and such law-breaking history loves and God blesses! Who says, then, that slave laws are not ten thousand times worse than any those men resisted? Whatever argument *excuses* them, makes John Brown a saint.[33]

But the opposition to slavery was not primarily a matter of the sentiments of humanity; it enlisted the deeds of humanity. The incredible accomplishment of Harriet Tubman in leading slaves to freedom and the highly efficient operation of the Underground Railroad exemplify civil disobedience in the grand manner. So much of the history of civil disobedience is the harrowing story of individuals against entrenched power or of heroism wasted that it is valuable to be able to include instances of disobedience carried off with a certain flair. Professor Madden, in his account of antislavery activity at Oberlin, tells the story of the Wellington Rescue case of 1858:

A runaway slave named John was captured and quickly taken to Wellington. John and his captors stayed at the Wadsworth House waiting for the next train out of northern Ohio. Students, faculty, and townspeople, hearing the news, spontaneously rushed to Wellington and through sheer numbers managed to rescue John without violence. But federal authority had been blatantly flouted, and the United States District Court of Cleveland took immediate action. Numerous Oberlinites were indicted, including Professor Henry Peck, associate professor of intellectual and moral philosophy, and James M. Fitch, superintendent of the Oberlin Sunday School. The arrest and trial attracted international attention. . . . The Oberlin community, however, had no intention of permitting the Wellington Rescuers to be sacrificed. The four slave-catchers were indicted for kidnaping before the Common Pleas Court of Lorain County. Clearly this court would be as completely Republican as the Cleveland court was completely Democratic. An exchange of convictions was the last thing the Southerners wanted, so both indictments were dropped and an exchange of prisoners was effected.[34]

Despite eloquence and courage, the promise of emancipation was not fulfilled to the American Negro. The pledge of the American dream was unrealized for women, for children, for the immigrants—thirty million of whom arrived between 1855 and 1915. The half century following the Civil War presented a great deal of unfinished business to a nation which had promised so much but was able to deliver on its promise only very unevenly. It was a period of growth, industrialization, and brawling tumult. It saw unprecedented corruption as well as a remarkable stir of reform. "Time would fail" to tell of the courageous challenges to existing order which marked the decades leading to the present. The purpose of this brief section has only been to indicate that civil disobedience is not a recent interloper, but an integral part of the teaching and practice of the American tradition.

Perhaps one strain remains to be remarked. The issues in which the civil disobedience hitherto described was employed were largely successful. The cause of the disobedients ultimately was vindicated. But a strongly developed tradition of civil disobedience has been present since the colonial period which has been less fortunate; its contribution must be measured in other ways. All through American history—from the witness of John Woolman to the voyage of the "Golden Rule" —there have been those pacifists who have taken what measures were available to register their fundamental objection to warfare and to their own participation in it. Some of their protest has simply been refusal to engage in killing. Some of their protest has been for the recognition of conscientious objection in legal procedures which are not humiliating. And some has been a protest against war itself. In maintaining this protest, the laws of a state which is the organizing vehicle for warfare have been deliberately broken. The pacifist witness has had

minor successes in winning recognition of the rights of conscientious objections. But in its longer quest for a world without war and a nation without militarism, the pacifist cause has
not prevailed. Yet the witness given and the cost borne have
not been useless. In recent generations the modern world has
shown a rising tolerance to horror and destruction. Those who
maintain absolute pacifism and who will take whatever steps
are necessary to dramatize their protest have a valuable (if
often a costly and unappreciated) role. Their refusal to acquiesce in the activities of a warfare state is a constant rebuke
and judgment. If their willingness to disobey keeps an uneasi-
ness alive in the national conscience, it serves an essential
calling, even though the pacifists themselves wish for something more.

These two chapters cannot pretend to be more than a highly
personal selection of words and events in the tradition of dissent
—a sort of idiosyncratic "Booke of Martyrs." Yet even this
rapid review will perhaps have made the point that the modern
world and the modern church are richer for the heritage of
godly disobedience.

five

: :

THE OBEDIENCE
WHICH MUST DISOBEY

It is necessary to ask now, given this biblical and historical inheritance, "Can Christians sense a responsible calling under God for today as Christians in the best moments of the church's past have discovered a faithful vocation under very different conditions? How can the question of civil disobedience be thought out constructively for our modern situation?"

In order to pursue such a question, we must begin with large, ultimate commitments which would be acknowledged by the community professing Christian faith. Without such an appeal to fundamentals, it would be difficult to adopt an attitude towards civil disobedience. (For civil disobedience is in itself only an instrument of political action. Like any other tool, it does (within the limits of its own nature) whatever a user makes it do. In order to determine whether or not it is a valuable tool, one must ask whether the thing done with it is worth doing and whether it is a thing best done in that way.)

No one practices deliberate, public, conscientious disobedience of a law he believes is good. Anyone engaged in such disobedience is persuaded that he acts under some higher law and against intolerable injustice. One might venture that many of the differences over civil disobedience are not so much differences over whether in principle evil laws should be opposed as they are differences over which laws are evil—or at least which are evil enough to warrant open noncompliance. We show shock at the illegalities of others, and we justify our own. Civil disobedience can be used by convinced partisans on

78

both sides of a question. It has been used for and against racial desegregation. Similarly (if one may make a point by setting side by side matters of such unequal seriousness), disobedience of established law was a factor in securing the adoption of Prohibition, and it was a factor in securing its repeal. Moreover, disobedience to established law may seem a viable tactic in a given cause at one point but not in that same cause at another time. Those who seek racial unity can at one time use "law and order" as allies while illegal activity is resorted to by segregationists. At another time, civil disobedience may be used as a weapon to challenge racial barriers maintained by law, while the opposition is crying "law and order." Yet this shift of ground will not seem inconsistent to those who must make it. Overriding moral purposes are served in one situation by obedience and in another by disobedience. The attitude to the law in either case would be justified by loyalty to that higher moral commitment. One cannot judge the rightness or wisdom of civil disobedience in the abstract. Rather one must ask specifically: "Disobedience against what? In behalf of what? From the point of view of what ethical mandates and political principles are you arguing that civil disobedience is a permissible tactic? Does your defense of disobedience take adequate account of the just claim of law, and does it pose the painful conflict of loyalties realistically?" A discussion of civil disobedience must be set in the context of such large inquiries as these.

Moralists and political theorists who have sanctioned civil disobedience have done so because of something in their thinking which makes civil law not the final determiner of right. In one idiom or another, they would echo Thoreau's dictum: "I think we should be men first, and subjects afterward." Humanism of this sort has made heroes; it has informed and nourished courage to defy oppressive laws and systems. Outside the most doctrinaire totalitarianisms, some such transcendence of man as man over man as citizen would be recognized.

The Christian community, for its part, would want to say

as much as the humanist says, but it would have its own way of saying it, and it would want to go on to say something more. In its internal discourse, the Christian community must theologize. It would regard man as most fully man when he is in conscious relation to the living God—a relation which may be vital apart from religious forms (and sterile in the midst of religious profession) and a relation which is never known except in a partial, culturally conditioned way. The God of Christian faith is held to disclose himself and his purposes in the whole of creation and history, but specifically in revelatory events and supremely in Jesus Christ. This disclosure provides certain points—in history, experience, and hope—to which Christian thinking makes constant reference. A determination of Christian obedience in the political order must proceed from these most immediate and basic realities of Christian faith.

THE CHURCH AS CHRIST'S PEOPLE

It may be useful to begin by restating the distinctiveness— the "strangeness"—of the Christian fellowship. The church is identified in the writings which account for its origin and character as a people called by God out of sin, darkness, and death into his own righteousness, and life. The church is the new people in Christ—bound up in a single fellowship uniting the sundered fragments of the human family. It is dependent on its Lord for its very existence and for its continued sustenance. Such familiar affirmations are not set down here as axioms for an argument; they are issues of faith and obedience. As the Confessing Church in Germany formulated its own understanding in the era of Nazism: "Jesus Christ, as he is attested for us in Holy Scripture is the one Word of God which we have to hear and which we have to trust and obey in life and in death." [1]

Such a reminder of the essential identity of the church as Christ's people—a reminder which, perhaps necessarily, con-

tinues to use biblical, traditional images—is not a retreat from
current, relevant matters. It is an orientation to primary realities. Perhaps in times calling for action or nonconformity the
church needs more than ever to know who it is. Perhaps when
its actual life is divided, weak, and compromised, it needs to
know what it is called to become. A reminder of its distinctiveness as the people of Christ may be the most relevant of all
possible affirmations if by it the church can bring to urgent
moral-political issues something not otherwise represented.

The Priority of God

As a people constituted in Christ, the church has learned
from its Lord to recognize the priority of God as the basic
reality of creed and life. The Old Testament faith in which
Jesus was nurtured and which he ratified affirmed: "Hear, O
Israel, the Lord our God is One Lord, and you shall love the
Lord your God with all your heart, and with all your soul,
and with all your might." [2] Jesus' own life was lived from the
Father, sustained by trust in the Father, nourished by obedience
to the Father's will, shared uniquely with the Father, and
rendered to the Father. God's Kingdom was the pearl of such
worth that everything else should be sold for it.[3] Jesus lived
and taught the total, exclusive Lordship of God.

The God of Jesus (and of Jewish faith) was the transcendent God who, though he is in all things, is yet maker of
all things who exists also in the Sabbath beyond the created
world. He is at work in history and uses all nations for his
purposes, but he is Lord of history and is identified ultimately
with the political fortune of no nation. He acts in ways only
partially discernible. He breaks upon men's plans when least
expected. His rebukes and his mercies are unpredictable; they
confound the wisdom of the wise.[4]

For his part, man's highest dignity, as disclosed in Christ,
is in the absolute recognition of the claim of God. He is to
look with a single eye (Matthew 6:22–24). He presses on,

hoping to take hold of that for which Christ once took hold of him (Philippians 3:12). He is to deny himself, take up his cross, and keep on following Christ. But this disciplined, concentrated service, this cross, this bond-service is not the restriction of full humanity. The service of God is man's perfect fulfillment and freedom.

The recognition of God's Lordship brings to human life a promise which is not made good within the conditions of history. God's acts remain incomplete; his faithfulness remains to be vindicated. Meantime, the church, in the ascended Christ, lives in history by the powers of the age to come. The church's true commonwealth is in heaven; its final destiny is with Christ beyond history. The church's present task is not to be large or influential so as to bring about the perfect ordering of things. The pledge to human life given in Jesus Christ will only be accomplished by Jesus Christ. The church is required to be faithful to its ultimate Lord and—in the midst of the fragmentariness of history—to live with the expectancy of a pilgrim.

These are the fundamental realities of biblical religion: the unconditional claim of God and the unqualified acquiescence of man.

This supreme claim implies the rejection of any rival claim which would usurp the obedience which is due to God and God alone. "Thou shalt have no other gods before me" is the First Commandment. The constant polemic of the Old Testament is against that most pathetic and futile but most persistent and versatile of human tendencies: idolatry. Man, in his perversity, seems endlessly resourceful in organizing his actual life values around his personal and group loyalties, his ideals, his ideologies, his tastes, his compulsions—and letting the forms of his religion (even biblically derived religion) sanction his actual commitment to a false, demeaning, enslaving god. Jesus rejected the temptation to misdirected allegiance by citing out of his tradition: "You shall worship the Lord your God and him only shall you serve." This is the first and greatest and most joyful—but most difficult—requirement of man.

The implications for civil disobedience of this supreme claim of God are the substance of the remainder of this chapter. But here it might be briefly noted that when a state claims for itself the ultimate prerogatives or the absolute homage which belong to God alone or when it prohibits or restricts the worship which is rightly due to God alone, it has overstepped its role and must be defied.

The Service of Neighbor

The same church which learns from Christ the priority of God learns also from the same Lord the claim, under God, of man. The Christ who lived and taught the unconditional grace and claim of God was not taken away from involvement in the human community by his recognition of that claim. He practiced unfailing, self-giving love for others. He came not to be ministered to, but to minister. He was, in Bishop Robinson's familiar adaptation of Dietrich Bonhoeffer's phrase, "the man for others." [5]

His calling to minister to others he shares with his church. He is Servant-Lord of a Servant-People.

When he had washed their feet, and taken his garments, and resumed his place, he said to them, "Do you know what I have done to you? You call me Teacher and Lord; and you are right, for so I am. If I then, your Lord and Teacher, have washed your feet, you also ought to wash one another's feet. For I have given you an example, that you should do as I have done to you. Truly, truly, I say to you, a servant is not greater than his master." (John 13:12–16)

According to the New Testament, this self-giving service is to have the quality of the unconditional, universal love of God who makes his favor (like his severity, Luke 13:1–5) fall on the worthy and the unworthy alike (Matthew 5:44f.). Human charity tends toward exclusiveness. We find it relatively easy to show kindness toward those with whom we feel a sense of kinship. Self-giving love is corrupted into collective egoism. But the love which is informed and judged by its rootage in God is required to transcend the "sense of kind" within which love tends to be confined. It is to exceed the righteousness of the calculating scribe. As H. Richard Niebuhr once expressed it: "Universal loyalty does not express itself as loyalty to the loyal but to whatever is; not a reverence for the reverent but a reverence for being; not as the affirmation of world affirmers but as world affirmation." [6]

Though God's love and purposes are universal, he does use human collectivities in the providential ordering of human affairs. It would be exceedingly foolish to argue that particular human loves must be the enemy of universal love or that God's large purposes are accomplished apart from kinship, religious, national, ethnic, community, economic groupings. These inevitable social units of human life are agents of history and the Lord of history. But each is required to relate its own intensive community sense and its own particular gifts to the larger purposes of the human community for whose sake each is created and called. The love learned in participation in the close sharing of like-minded people must be fulfilled, enlarged, and corrected by a wider unity and sharing with all.

A universal, self-giving love at work in a divided world will be a force for reconciliation. The church is called to represent in history the "one new man" which is human community reconstituted in Christ. The "middle walls of partition" which men build and cherish cannot be recognized by community established in Christ. A great theologian has commented that the fellowship of grace "has no frontiers except those it exists to remove." [7]

The church, moreover, ministers in the name of one who is life and who came to bring life. It must, in his name, oppose all that restricts, all that oppresses, all that deceives, destroys, and kills. God in Christ has declared that he is *for us*—graciously and forever. Before we could in any way respond, we were objects of his favor. This is the wonder of the gospel which creates the church and its confidence. "If God be for us, who can be against us?" (Romans 8:31) And, as God is *for man,* the church must be clearly and unfailingly *for man.*

Practical Applic

The immediate implications for civil disobedience of this claim of man are clear. When a state adopts a policy that treats men as less than fully human, it must be opposed. This general statement requires fuller clarification and qualification; but the presumption is clear from the Christian faith that, in the name of man, governmental action which excludes, divides, brutalizes, or depersonalizes may be subject to moral censure and conscientious noncompliance. The Christian community may have to become the enemy of a state which has made itself the enemy of man.

The Interdependence of the Two Claims

It has already been suggested that these two claims—the claim of God and the claim of man—are not rivals. The second commandment is "like unto" and inseparable from the first. Loyalty to Jesus Christ is not adequately expressed in a pietism unrelated to criticism of and commitment to the social order. Neither is loyalty to Jesus Christ represented by a humanitarianism which stands apart from the constraint and corrective of the love of God (or which regards the reality of God as optional while cherishing a high regard for Jesus as a model of service).

The point is obvious enough but worth making explicit here, for in several traditions it has been thought that churches need raise no objection to political despotism and state-sponsored inhumanity as long as the church's prerogatives—worship particularly, but also preaching, instruction, and evangelization—are not interfered with. But this drawing of lines is usually tactically self-defeating. A state determined on an unjust course will have been able to inflict a great deal of human damage before so docile a church needs to be reckoned with directly. By the time worship itself is restricted or forbidden, the momentum of the state will be so great and the compliance of the church so established by silence that belated opposition can accomplish little. Moreover, such opposition is weakened by its obvious defensive concern about the institutional church after a period of unconcern about man.

The two claims are parts of a whole. An attack on man and on the structures of justice needs to be recognized as an attack on that whole just as truly as if public worship were banned. Indeed, any piety which can survive intact and untroubled in the midst of social injustice betrays its own delusional quality. The ministry of the word and the sacraments sets the church in a society whose pain or well-being forms the very stuff of proclamation and offering.

THE PRESENCE OF THE OPPOSITION

God's purposes in Christ and his church must be worked out in a world which is sin-structured and by a church which itself has all the characteristics of division, self-centeredness, and blindness of the world for whose redemption it exists. A fundamental selfishness and rebellion mark every human life and institution. Every human achievement has its own traitor within the gates, ready to undo the best that has been accomplished. Man has an inveterate tendency to worship the works of his own hands—and to insist that others do so too. Man's communities tend to divide—victims of individual and collective vanity. Men tend to use the power they have to manage and exploit their brothers. Although the Christian faith requires that we recognize with gratitude real human altruism, generosity, and self-sacrifice, it will not let us settle for a superficial analysis of sin. William Temple, one of the best of men, once said: "I can be good if I want to: the trouble is that I don't want to." [8]

THE PLACE OF GOVERNMENT AND CIVIC DUTY

This brief sketch of the conditions of life and faith suggests the value and the necessity of human government. Man is capable of community; he has the unique ability to say "we," to pool his ideas, his dreams, his work, and to order his common life for the accomplishment of desired purposes. Therefore he needs a structuring of his society to provide the precondition for cooperative achievement. But man tends to destroy his own communities and to attack in predatory fashion the communities of others. Individuals rebel against the disciplined role of citizen which the community of justice demands. Therefore we need the devices of government to restrain the "war of everyone against everyone" into which unchecked self-will would plunge the human family.

These considerations suggest that responsible political thought and action belong to the very character of man. They are not optional; they are not a dirty business to be avoided whenever possible. They are constitutive of the dignity and meaning of man. They are among the most significant of human activities.

A Christian owes a specific duty to that social order and government within which he lives. Part of his ultimate loyalty to God is discharged through his proximate loyalty to the government which God himself has established in his providential rule of history. The ordered community, as older than the individual citizen, is the bearer of inherited symbols and is the vehicle of that structuring through which a person learns who he is. Life's largest questions use political and social experience in their exploration. Further, part of a Christian's service for his neighbor is fulfilled through his duties as citizen. Participation in the organized life of society enables one to take large responsibilities for the freedoms and well-being of the thousands of one's fellows with whom he is bound up in political jurisdictions. If the individual later becomes critical of his inherited political order and seeks to alter it or even to overthrow it, his critique probably owes most of its best points to the inheritance from which it arose, and the passion of the critique probably comes from a sense of outraged betrayal in the inconsistencies of one's immediate elders. It is here in this place and now in this time that I am set. This is "given." I was not consulted about it. It is in and through participation —grateful but not uncritical—in the affairs of this ordered community that I am called and enabled to serve the ultimate purposes of my existence. The supreme claim of citizenship in the commonwealth of heaven does not draw a Christian away from citizenship in the human community or make him indifferent to the condition of its members. Quite the contrary, a person of faith is given an inherent commitment to the human order and to the use of its political methods for the accomplishment of the possible good and the limitation of needless misery. Christians have an explicit duty to government.

LIMITATIONS ON THE CLAIM OF GOVERNMENT

But though the governments of the human community have a real claim on the Christian citizen, the claim is not unlimited. Though they can properly exact the discharge of important duties—even involving the citizen in major personal sacrifices for the common good—the rights of government are not unconditional. Governments were made for man, not man for governments. The proper function and dignity of government is as a means to the human good—a good which the state does not create or confer. A pastor and theologian in West Berlin has put it this way:

In making laws the state has to deal with men already associated together, with mutual obligations which it did not create, but which it should help to maintain, and which therefore are not to be disposed of as it sees fit, and which it cannot just disregard, but has to respect. . . . A state is a just state only as long as the power of the state respects these limitations.[9]

In short, the state is under an obligation to serve its people, to serve all its people, and to act honorably in their name in its relations with other nations.

THE SINS OF THE STATE

But there is a tendency of every human collectivity to serve itself. Governments especially—as wielders of control and coercion—are wont to mistake means for ends and to identify the good of the machinery of political power with the good of the people. Unchecked, the state tends to exceed its proper claims and competence, to recognize only a portion of society and identify with its interests, and to become aggressive or expansionist in its international role.

These Titanist tendencies are most obvious, of course, in the totalitarian states which usurp the place and prerogatives of God and reduce persons to creatures to be manipulated for the state's own purposes. John C. Bennett has commented of such states:

> The absolute state with its claim to be the source of truth, the determiner of the purposes of society, and the judge of culture is an enemy of Christ in every age. It must either deny God's existence or seek to make him over into its own image; it must either seek to destroy the Church or domesticate it for its own purposes.[10]

The corrupting tendency of power requires that Christian political theorists insist on the limited state.

A limited state is, among other things, a government of law. In a constitutional system, the government writes and administers laws under a freely adopted standard which both empowers the government and at the same time restricts its power. The government itself is governed. Power is distributed within the government and ultimately has its source not in the government but in the people. Government is not only a force to restrain the citizen; the citizenry can restrain the government. But both these restraints ought to be exercised through law rather than as the unreflective acts of officials or factions. The laws are checks on the arbitrariness of governmental action and on the caprice of individual or popular impulse. Laws are thus the indispensable bonds of political community. They deserve respect. But they can only fill their necessary function in the community and retain the community's respect if they are— in form and operation—inclusive and impartial. That is, no person or group should be allowed to rise above the restraints of the laws, and no person or group should be allowed to fall below the equal protection of the laws.

Such is the intention of a limited state. It represents in theory a great human aspiration. And in the practice which approximates that dream, it has allowed for free and responsible citizenship, for initiative to meet new circumstances and correct old abuses, and for a fulfilling human life in a community governed lightly and without oppression. But in some societies and under some ideologies, of course, the idea itself is rejected. Even where the dream is cherished, it expects of citizens more intelligence and disinterestedness than are always available. Further, even in a state with representational structures and careful checks and balances, the proper business of government can be betrayed by those who are entrusted with that business. As Carl Becker once said, "To suppose that because we have a government of laws we have not a government of men is a misleading and dangerous fallacy." [11] The capturing of political power, the retention of it, and the use of its authority for a faction's own interests become all-consuming passions. Either in design or execution, free, constitutional government is often clumsily carried out.

This corruption of a political ideal is not always a result of deliberate decision or extreme depravity. Persons of good intentions who mean to support equality and justice will yet have access to only a partially informed idea of what justice may be. Laski put the matter:

Men think differently who live differently; and in the approach to the problem of what legal imperatives are ultimately desirable in the interests of the community as a whole, each class approaches the question with an unstated and half-conscious major premise at the back of its mind which is of fundamental importance to its view of reason or justice. Rich men always underestimate the power of property to secure happiness; religious men always overestimate the influence of faith upon morals; learned men usually attach undue importance to the relation of scholarship to wisdom. We are the prisoners of our experience. . . . Power depends for its habits upon a consciousness of possession, a habit of organization, an ability to produce an immediate effect. In a democratic state, where there are great inequalities of economic power, the main characteristics of the poor are exactly the want of these.[12]

Through some such forces, the political structure of the community becomes the tool of the dominant group and is used to favor its interests—often without intending actual injustice.

A further problem for the limited state is that in a populous, urban, technologically developed society, the involvement of government and people becomes greater and the character of a "limited state" harder to define. As the government—often for humane reasons—takes some responsibility in more aspects of life, the possibility of its exceeding its proper role as a political instrument becomes greater. Similarly, as a vigorous government seeks to assume some responsibility for defense, human welfare, and economic strength in other nations, the possibility of domination of weaker peoples becomes greater. The determination of a proper role for government—never an easy matter—becomes exceedingly difficult in our time. The possibilities for both good and ill are greatly extended in the large behemothlike structures of the superstates brought into being by our complex world.

THE INDIVIDUAL JUDGMENT ON THE STATE

As an exercise of full personhood, a man must not just accept on authority whatever his government or culture decrees. He must question. A man who simply echoes the crowd or repeats the conventional wisdom is not taking responsibility for his individual, singular identity. He is letting himself be determined by mass influences in his environment; he is not affirming himself against them and agreeing or disagreeing from the depths of his own judgment.[13] He has allowed other forces to assume control of himself at that profound level of existence at which one is answerable to God alone.

An individual's consideration of his government's contentions may lead him to reject the dictates of the state. The Nuremburg trials at the end of World War II (though their legal status is equivocal) were a way of saying that a man cannot exonerate himself by a plea that he did an evil act on orders from higher up. One must accept individual responsibility for moral decisions. But the individual's consideration might also lead to concurrence in the dictates of the state. In this case, however, the individual will not have been passive. He will, on his own, have investigated the merits of the case and accepted obedience as a free, responsible choice. In a democratic society, the best kind of loyalty to the state is that which never ceases to be skeptical, critical, responsible, and intelligent; and the best kind of community is that which recognizes and cherishes informed dissent.

When faced with what he takes, at first glance, to be official folly, how does a Christian citizen engage in responsible questioning?

Some Qualifications for the Individual Critic

A number of possible answers come to mind which, among them, may well cover many of the cases of conscientious criticism.

When one supposes the state to be in the wrong, he can remember the complexity of most public questions and the limitations of his own information and viewpoint, and he can consider that there may be factors unknown to him which would put the action of the government in a more favorable light.

Or one can engage, through the formal and informal processes of democratic society, in actions which register his disagreement. When this is attempted, the effort might prevail. Many landmarks in the revision of government policy have begun as private protest. The effort, however—as far as anyone can see at the time—might fail.

In that case, the graceful course, in most instances, is for the citizen simply to acquiesce and follow the majority. Many thousands of persons who were, as matters of grave personal principle, opposed to the adoption of social security or to the repeal of prohibition or who were for the retention of Bible reading in public schools have accepted defeat as far as national practice is concerned—though they may often continue private, organized representation of their opinions. The corollary of a one-man, one-vote rule by majority decision is that many persons must learn the role of defeated minorities. As long as the essential structures of equality and justice are sound, the defeat of a minority opinion need not place the holders in a position of indignity. Further, most persons are in a minority on some issues and with the majority on others. Democratic order does not mean that everyone gets just what he wants; it is a fabric of adjustments which citizens, as a mark of maturity, learn to accept.

In a democratic society, when a citizen identifies actions of the state which he regards as unjust or mistaken, he must ask himself about his own complicity in the government policy he deplores. The "state" and the "people" are so closely and responsibly linked that it is seldom a case of a guilty "they" clearly distinguishable from an innocent "we." Most public policies are maintained because a great many people find it to their advantage to have them maintained. Few individuals have a detached place of uninvolved, outraged innocence from which to condemn the government. Most persons are responsible, participating, articulate citizens bound together in a community of discourse and common actions and hence likely to be involved in "accessory guilt" when the political unit errs. The late

Edmond Cahn, in his splendid book *The Predicament of Democratic Man,* proposes a "citizen's self-search" for use by those who think their state committed to an immoral course. He suggests the citizen ask himself:

> Did I incite the official to commit a wrong?
> Did I authorize the wrong?
> Was I reckless in helping to install a conspicuously dangerous public instrument?
> Did I remain silent or passive when I might have prevented a wrong about to be perpetrated?
> Did I ratify the act of wrong or knowingly accept its fruits?
> Did I suppress the truth when it came to my notice and thus become an accessory after the fact?
> Before the wrong was committed, had I contributed to the vulnerability of the victim?

Cahn remarks of his own questions, "Fortunate is the citizen who, after considering them rigorously in the forum of his conscience, can exonerate himself on every count." [14] Such a self-search is not meant to indicate that there are no innocent, victimized groups or persons. It is not meant to suggest that in a democratic society every individual citizen is personally answerable for the follies of a nation of scores of millions of people. It is not meant to encourage a self-flagellation of the conscience which would paralyze criticism or action. The self-search would simply remind the citizen engaged in protest that, to the extent that he himself shares the guilt of his society, he must moderate the shrill, accusing tone that his protest might otherwise have. Right and wrong can still be distinguished; wrong can be protested and right championed. But it will all have to be done with the chastened passion of one who recognizes that the wrong he opposes is, in part, his own, and the right for which he speaks is, in his own case, not unspotted.

Some Vindications of the Individual Critic

But these considerations will not ease all questions a citizen might raise about his government. While it is true that public officials might have pertinent (and unsharable) information and a large perspective unavailable to the individual, it is also possible for an official, owing to his close involvement in the processes of government, to become blind to certain morally basic considerations; such close involvement may well shield him from the clarity that an issue has for persons not bound by previous official commitments. There is little reason to conclude that professional careers in politics, administrative office, or military life in themselves impart a wisdom about public affairs and national purposes superior to that attainable by an individual in "lay" status. Madison once said: "If we advert to the nature of republican government, we shall find that the censorial power is in the people over the government, and not in government over the people." [15] Just as a citizen might want to consider the possibility that he might be wrong and the government right, the very process of such consideration might also lead that citizen to the growing conviction that he is right and the government deeply wrong.

Similarly, it is possible for the citizen, or for many citizens acting unitedly, to feel that despite the freedom for protest granted in American society and despite some past success in changing governmental policy, the issue he is pressing is so drastic a challenge to existing commitments and their ideological supports that he stands little chance of getting a hearing. Further, even if there is hope of changing laws and policies by the moral force of one's argument or of righting injustice through appeal to courts, the process is inevitably long, expensive, and full of uncertainties. Meantime, in the view of the protesting person or group, the life-destroying or community-destroying condition persists. Under a sense of urgency, those who protest are often faced with the question: Will the harm that may be done by a direct challenge (even to the point of deliberate lawbreaking) which may force the community's attention to long overdue reform be greater than the harm that will most certainly be done by allowing the well-established injustice to continue destroying persons and poisoning the social order until the usual, gradual processes of institutional change have done their work?

Further, it is to be feared that the gradual processes do not bring about improvement automatically. Time is on the side of the existing status unless some important force breaks the inertia. It is possible for some individual persons to rise above their personal background and situation and identify and protest injustices which do not bring direct harm on themselves. They can genuinely align themselves with wronged persons just because they are wronged and be outraged by social immorality just because it is immoral. However, these large-spirited individuals seldom can, in themselves, effect change in laws and procedures. Their social passion cannot be imparted to groups gathered around special interests. Most once-revolutionary groups, having gained the point which brought them into self-conscious existence, retain their identity, but with a stake now in the maintenance of the existing system. Idealism alone is unlikely to dislodge a static pattern. Community injustices which are extensive and long-maintained have usually been of some long-range benefit to the advantaged portion of the society—the portion which tends to have in its control the law-writing and law-enforcing apparatus as well as the (purportedly free) instruments of communication and public suasion. Such a favored group does not yield or share its position gladly just in the interest of some abstract formulation of justice. No dominant group is likely to reform itself out of its favored position. There is no tendency of history which checks oppressors automatically. Concessions must be wrung from advantaged groups slowly and painfully. The effort can expect to meet indifference at best, and brutal, unprincipled opposition at worst. In order to win a point against entrenched injustice, there must be courage, determination, a willingness to absorb pain and, above all, a combination of morality and power. Without the power, the moral right can be disregarded —indeed, eloquent protest apart from power can be encouraged by the advantaged group as a harmless means of releasing the outraged passion of wronged persons. As long as it is not linked with power, it constitutes no threat and need not be taken seriously. If these observations describe the realities of political life with even approximate truth, it is folly to counsel the use of the channels open to representative government as a means to change laws apart from the "muscle" which tends to enliven the conscience of legislators. It might be constructive to request, from those who counsel that only courts and legislatures be used for hearing protest, some evidence that such counsel is given in the interest of equal justice rather than in the interest of using "the law's delay" to keep social control in the hands of the dominant group, which will grant as a concession that which is a basic right—and grant it (if at all) at a time and in a manner of the dominant group's determination. In the world of serpents, it is fatal to be uniformly dove-like. Moral passion alone is not enough. The passage of time in itself solves nothing. The democratic process is not automatic in its recognition and remedy of injustice. Those who wish to right social wrongs must take initiative themselves which will be recognized by the government itself as representing actual or potential power.

Of course, the stress between conscientious citizen and his government has, in our time, become more intolerable than even the foregoing comments have indicated. It is possible for governments to pursue explicit destructive policies whose first victims are portions of its own people. Such a situation prevailed in the Third Reich in Germany, and resistance to the state was the course to which many persons were led as a matter of Christian obedience. In portions of the United States, governments have committed themselves openly and energetically to the repression of Negroes, the extermination or isolation of other minority groups. But governmental inaction which allows an oppressive condition to continue can be just as intolerable as direct governmental aggression. In the minds of many persons, the failure of the governments of the most affluent nation on earth to undertake more than ineffective, token steps to remedy the lot of the ill-housed, undernourished, badly educated, underemployed, discriminated-against quarter of its population can be ascribed to nothing short of deliberate decision to do nothing about it. The persons relegated to this "other America" are unfulfilled, hopeless, and despairing. Their life expectancy is actually shorter than the national average by a significant number of years. The nation seems to many persons to be, by its governmental complacency (reflecting doubtless a general complacency) and inaction, violating systematically the command of the supreme Lawgiver: "Thou shalt not kill." Similarly, a sizable portion of the American population has felt that no account of the American military action in Vietnam has yet been put forward which would begin to justify the staggering force being employed and the damage, suffering, and death (civilian and military, American and Vietnamese, northern and southern) being inflicted. Lacking such an account, citizens have inquired for themselves and, in many instances, are persuaded that their nation is committed to a moral disaster course.

WHEN THE CRITIC MUST ACT

Persons who are sensitive to these conditions in this way now must ask: "What am I to do when—after full consideration—I am convinced that my government is wrong, terribly wrong, on a matter of major importance and that it is requiring me to be an accomplice in its evil?" Sharp issues of conscience are being posed. Many persons are being asked to participate in actions which they regard as oppressive, unjust, and destructive—and they cannot. Others are being asked to accept roles which they believe demean their essential human dignity —and they will not.

The government cannot expect (and Christian spokesmen

ought not to defend) absolute assent to its acts regardless of its ability to argue their moral merits. In a free society, dissent is to be expected; and the government must be in dialogue with its critics. Sacrifices called for by the state must be voluntarily assumed by a free and responsible citizenry which finds the case made for these sacrifices to be compelling and to carry general moral authority. Only God can claim, as of right, absolute obedience. To give to government the kind of unquestioning assent that belongs to God alone is the crassest idolatry. Many Christians are convinced that the government has overstepped its proper role and asked them to do things it is not competent to ask and sought to prevent them from doing things it is not competent to forbid. Such persons feel that they must now affirm God by denying the state.

Neither can the government expect the willing cooperation of citizens when, in the minds of many, the actions or inactions of government inflict or ignore human suffering. Many members of the Christian community have become convinced that they must affirm man by denying the state. The loyalties now felt by many Christians shape themselves rather like those articulated by Dietrich Bonhoeffer:

The crucified Christ has become the refuge and the justification, the protection and the claim for the higher values and their defenders that have fallen victim to suffering. It is with the Christ who is persecuted and who suffers in His Church that justice, truth, humanity and freedom now seek refuge; it is with the Christ who found no shelter in the world, the Christ who was cast out from the world, the Christ of the crib and the cross under whose protection they now seek sanctuary, and who thereby for the first time displays the full extent of His power.[16]

For all of the history of the American people (and for much of the history of the Christian community since A.D. 313) it has been possible for the bulk of the professing Christian community (though probably always with a measure of self-deception) to regard national or civic pieties and Christian faith as reconcilable if not, indeed, identical. But the church is entering on a new epoch when such assumptions would be naïve. Christian consciences are becoming newly alert to the damage (to the gospel, the church, and the nation) of comfortable, culturally determined religion. Tensions are felt where they were not a few years ago. Formerly acceptable styles of Christian life and community are now intolerable for many discerning persons.

In our fragmented society and our divided, class-identified and race-identified churches, groups will differ as to how far they think this growing opposition has advanced. Individuals will differ as to how critical they regard the conflict as having become for their own consciences in their specific situations. But anyone who can imagine that the claims of Christ might be heard *against* the claims of the state must recognize that our times contain those conditions which are likely to produce conscientious Christian civil disobedience. Christians may, in considerable numbers, feel themselves called to witness to the supremacy of Christ for their consciences through acts of disobedience to the conflicting demands of civil authority.

When the issue shapes itself in that way, a Christian has no real choice; *he must disobey.* The form of the disobedience may vary all the way from quiet individual noncompliance to large scale defiance. The opportunities and limitations of each specific situation need to determine. But tactical matters are another discussion. Here we have considered only the decision to disobey and the grounds on which such a decision might be reached. We cannot have represented this decision rightly if we have failed to suggest that the process of coming to it involves conflict, pain, and cost. But whatever the cost of defying the state in the name of Christ, the cost, for a Christian, of prudential assent to the expectations of the state, when they are contrary to what he takes to be the will of Christ, is incalculably greater.

six
: :
THE CONDITIONS OF
RESPONSIBLE DISOBEDIENCE

The civil disobedience which is part of Christian obedience is not irresponsible. It is not undertaken lightly. It is so serious a matter that some conditions or restraints should be indicated.

In the tumultuous times in which civil disobedience is seriously considered by any large number of people, there is little opportunity for weighing alternatives and making a mental check of a list of conditions which ethicists might want to see met. Decisions must be made quickly. Commitment must be given without the reflection that one might wish for. Emotions are sure to run high. The particular features of any specific situation can seem quite unlike the tidy situations for which guidelines were drawn up. A general analysis must seem abstract and above-the-battle to a participant who, with limited information and time, must make a venture which may carry ruinous consequences.

Yet discussion of qualifications and restraints is not beside the point. Christian action ought to be spontaneous and an affirmation of freedom under Christ, but it dare not be mindless. It must be something with a meaning which can be articulated—even if not fully.

Moreover, an action such as deliberate disobedience of a law on Christian grounds ought to be done in a community of discussion, understanding, and support. A person who makes an appeal to conscience may find himself isolated. Antigone was not ashamed "to think alone." But the individual who must act should be able to bring to his acting a background of discussion or a "sense of the meeting" from that community to which he has looked for guidance in establishing for himself an ethical stance. The discussion may not always be completely applicable or useful. Each person must take ultimate responsibility and act on his own. The decisions made by persons acting in conscience become in turn new data for the ongoing corporate discussion and its provisional ethical formulations. The community's general understanding is not an absolute; it is a growing, adapting thing. The individual and the community, the concrete action and the general community-search for consensus on the issue must interact.

Thus, the following considerations are not meant as a checklist for the individual or the group which must, under pressure, decide and live by the consequences of its decision. In specific situations, certain considerations take on overwhelming intensity while others seem unimportant; a general, academic body of qualifications would only be of limited value if their function was misunderstood. The following considerations are intended principally for the thinking processes of the community which corporately must help to first "count the cost" and then give counsel and support.

A Calculus of Evil

A primary condition has been indicated in the previous chapter. Before a person can justifiably violate a law he disagrees with, he ought to be convinced that the harm that might be done (to himself and to the community) by such an act would be less than the harm (to himself and to the community) of continued conformity to what he considers to be a bad law. There are many laws and procedures in a modern state which a citizen might regard as unwise or irksome; he wishes they were other than they are. But many of these regulations are of a trivial sort involving no deep issue of conscience. To protest them by explicit disobedience would exaggerate their importance—and probably betray the exaggerated importance the protester attached to himself as well. Robert Meyners comments of a Christian:

> Since he is realistic about the destructive possibilities of anarchy, he will not oppose the existing order for insignificant reasons. No historical order even approximates the ideal social order which he knows to be the will of God. The fact that the existing order is imperfect is by itself never any grounds for opposing it. The costs and the dangerous possibilities of resistance are such that the existing order must be significantly worse than it may reasonably be expected to be, and so significantly worse as to justify the risks involved in resistance.[1]

But many issues are of the highest importance for the conscience of one who is being required to participate in injustice. For a young man who may not be a doctrinaire pacifist to be asked to take up arms in an undeclared war which, according to his information, has been overwhelmingly condemned by world opinion, a war in which, in his opinion, his own nation has repeatedly violated the 1949 Geneva Conventions on the conduct of warfare and the treatment of civilians and prisoners, a war which, in his judgment, fails on many counts the traditional conditions of a "just war," becomes, for that person, a matter of deepest conscience. Similarly, to be required to observe racial laws and customs (either as the discriminator or the discriminated against) is in itself a violation of a Christian conscience which regards racism in all its forms as the "most dangerous myth" of the modern world. Persons who feel that profound issues of conscience are at stake in such decisions sense that a cost is involved in disobedience. There may be personal indignities visited on one; there may even be government-tolerated violence and government-inflicted imprisonment. There can be a real jeopardizing of one's future career. If enough people feel strongly on such matters and act with obvious integrity and courage, their convictions could begin to modify public opinion and policy. But there is no assurance that such an impact would register on the community. In a strongly polarized community, the ability of a dominant group to bully objectors and show its contempt for those it takes to be cowards, nonconformists, or do-gooders is not to be minimized. Protest—even if by a large number of persons—could leave the community more hardened in its course than it was before the challenge was mounted. All of these matters must be weighed. And yet many persons will feel that the cost of civil disobedience and the unknown consequences of it are less than the cost of continued acquiescence in injustice with its certain perpetuation of loss and suffering for others and intolerable compromise for oneself.

The Affirmation of Law

A Christian breaking of a law must be in the name of law. In other words, civil disobedience, to be Christian, ought to be basically an affirmation of law. When one identifies a specific positive law as defective and protests it to the point of noncompliance, he cannot responsibly do so as a step toward a mythical state of nature in which men and communities are free from all external regulation. The correction for the abuse of law is not the removal of all laws. A badly ordered community is not made more humane and civilized by dispensing with order entirely. Law, in a general sense, is not the opposite of freedom; it is the precondition of freedom. It allows persons to develop individually and work unitedly with a minimum of conflict. Laws, however, can accomplish this beneficent purpose only if they are themselves informed by some general understanding of human dignity and the purposes of human community. It is in this general sense that a "law of humanity" is sometimes spoken of as that which must be embodied in the written laws of the community. Appeal can be made, with moral dignity, from positive laws of the community written in violation of such informing principles to that "higher law" itself. When specific laws are opposed, a Christian cannot substitute only a nihilistic rejection of law; he must commend instead laws which are a better approximation of that law of humanity which he cherishes. Of the conscientious breakers of laws, Thoreau once said: "They are the lovers of law and order who observe the law when the government breaks it." [2]

Though some such appeal is probably implicit in Christian (and perhaps in all) statements of civil disobedience, the Christian faith is bound to no single philosophical setting for this "higher law." The Christian community is able to make common cause with those who define it by revealed doctrines, natural moral law, philosophical idealism, self-evident truths about man, or just by superior workability. But in her own understanding of man, the source of the Christian community's "law of humanity" by which positive laws and political schemes are affirmed and judged is the church's concrete experience of God in Jesus Christ. In him there is an inexhaustible resource for the renewal of human life and community. To be sure, this concrete experience is not itself a political principle; it does not provide quick and ready judgments about specific laws and political arrangements. But in this encounter with God in Christ as redemption and judgment, the church knows itself to have met also the one who is ground and criterion of every human life and community. To be faithful to this constitutive factor in Christian belief, every act of civil disobedience must be at the same time both a negation of a civil law and an affirmation of Jesus Christ—the one in whom "all things are held together." [3]

American society has had a tendency toward excessive confidence in laws. For a social difficulty, we have said, "There ought to be a law." We have supposed that the passage of a law disposes of a matter. We attach great significance to formal legality even though we have been a violent, ill-disciplined nation. We know no graceful middle ground between, on the one hand, an awed sense of the "sacredness" of law and, on the other hand, a cynical evasion of and contempt for laws.

If Christian faith can bring a corrective to this state of mind, it may be by helping a legalistically inclined society to be somewhat less tightly and rigidly attached to laws themselves and somewhat more faithful to the bonds of community which are more basic than those created by acts of legislatures. Along such lines, Reinhold Niebuhr once wrote:

There is a tendency among Christians, as well as non-Christians, to retire to the security of law, and to forget that even the best laws may become the servant of interest and sin. . . . Unless divine grace flow into the heart, men will not only fail to obey the law but will use it as an instrument for their own advantage. Christian legalism has helped to sow confusion into the chaos of our day. The cure for modern lawlessness is not more emphasis upon law or efforts to define specific laws more sharply. The cure of modern lawlessness is to bring the idolatry and self-worship of all men and nations under divine judgment and to free men from both law and sin so that all things may be theirs if they are Christ's. In that spirit they can create not an anarchistic millennium but communities, and constantly renew and refresh them by the spirit of love.[4]

When a Christian concludes that he must violate a specific law, he does not do it as an act of disrespect for law as such but as an act of obedience to and witness for that gospel which is guarantor and judge of all true law, true humanity, and true community.

Usually a Last Resort

Ordinarily a Christian would only enter on a course of civil disobedience after all other ways short of that extremity had been tried and found ineffective. The intentional violation of a law is so shocking a thing for the fabric of laws and community order that it should not be used as a tactic if the ends in view can be gained in other, more gradual ways.

However, this condition cannot be pressed too categorically. Exceptional conditions may modify its general applicability. Some persons are in situations of such urgency that their opportunities to explore alternatives to civil disobedience are quite restricted. They have only time enough to react—with little reflection—to a demand which they cannot but think it incumbent for them not to obey. Again, as Father Robert Drinan, Dean of Boston College Law School, has pointed out, "there are some injustices which, even if eventually they will be corrected, are so inherently shameful that those who suffer them have a right to exercise self-help." [5] The wait for the exhausting of all alternatives would prolong an intolerable situation. Moreover, since a person faced with a law he questions is seldom alone in questioning it, the community of his fellows can often go through the process of trying the alternatives to civil disobedience and finding them futile. The individual can accept and draw on their prior experience. Each concerned person need not exhaust all such possibilities individually. Further, to cite Father Drinan again:

> Some injustices . . . place their victims in such pain, humiliation and moral peril that the minority group inflicted by them, has not merely a right but conceivably a duty to bring them to public attention by some dramatic even spectacular conduct. The orderly processing of complaints through appropriate tribunals may therefore be the usual way of bringing justice to citizens. But non-white citizens whose burdens are manifestly extraordinary should not in all cases be required to wait for relief until an apathetic white majority becomes conscious of their grievances and ready to redress them.[6]

In sum, the opportunities and the necessity for the exploration of alternatives may not be great for each person in each situation, but to the extent that they are present they should be attempted.

But when peaceful, law-abiding protest has been tried and has failed to get a hearing, or when such protest is rendered impossible by high-handed manipulation of permissions and opportunities, or when the protesting persons are without genuine access to anyone who might grant relief, and when the offending law is such that an issue of basic conscience is clearly involved, then a deliberate violation of the law becomes not an impatient, irresponsible act, but a course now open as a last resort—and a judgment not only on the specific law in question, but on the restrictive character of the community which drives its conscientious citizens to such extremity.

The Identification of a Specific Aim

A responsible act of civil disobedience ought to have not only a general negative and constructive intent; it ought also to identify its specific aim. That is to say, it ought not to be a diffuse, irritated rejection of the establishment-and-all-its-works. It ought to grow out of an analysis of a specifiable wrong, and its protest should make clear what that wrong is. Limited gains are all that can be expected in the political realm, so it is desirable that one's aims be well enough defined so that it can be determined whether or not they have been attained.

Usually the issue will be embodied in a law which sanctions or authorizes the evil, and civil disobedience will take the form of breaking that law. Those who specifically object to the selective service system and laws, for example, will feel that their registering for the draft is itself a form of cooperation with the evil system. Their disobedience is designed to express the focus of their opposition.

But the situation is not always that simple. Sometimes there is no law where one is wanted—demonstrations for civil rights bills or for open-housing legislation deal with this sort of gap. In some cases a specific human grievance may exist though it is not apparently caused by an existing law, and those who feel the impact of the grievance should not themselves be expected to specify the terms of the ordinance which would relieve it. In still other cases, it is not the presence or the absence of a law which is at issue, but the procedures of administrative or enforcement officers who act under general

mandate of laws but whose work is primarily governed by
directives within an executive department.

In such cases, the act of civil disobedience cannot be direct
—no law is at issue. It must be indirect. That is to say, a law
may be broken which has an oblique relation to the grievance.
Perhaps a mayor's office is filled with persons who refuse to
leave at the close of business hours. They are not there protesting the right of the mayor and his staff to close the office
and go home at the end of a day; they are protesting some other
matter for whose existence and correction the mayor is regarded as the moving (or perhaps the nonmoving) force. The
"sit-in" in his honor's office is perhaps meant to call community attention to a problem or to provoke the mayor to
initiate legislation or administrative steps which will correct
the abuse. But such meaning will not be clear from the law
that is broken, nor from the manner of breaking it. Under
certain conditions, this indirect form of civil disobedience may
be all that is possible, and its use is quite defensible. But when
it is used, it is important that its intention be made clear. It
is likely to provoke misunderstanding and produce unwanted
consequences; caution and clarity are necessary.

A Concern for Means

A course of civil disobedience informed by Christian conscience must show responsibility for the means chosen to
achieve the desired ends. One's whole effort can founder
through the use of means out of harmony with the end
being sought.* Unless one is prepared to argue that the end
justifies the means, a great deal of discipline is called for at
this point. An inappropriate means can undo the beneficent
intention of the protest. The fact that violence has been visited

* This point concerning the appropriate means for civil disobedience
is so complicated and so important that the following chapter is devoted entirely to a discussion of it.

on a person or group does not (if Christian sanctions are to be drawn upon) permit the wronged party to use retaliatory violence in the name of putting down violence. Anger, intemperate remarks concerning one's opponent or actual, physical injury are all means which have an inner dialectic; they tend to run away with their user and corrupt the ground rules of his dealing with others; they tend to make those who feel their impact more resistant to change. Such excessive means may be used unintentionally because, in the stress of a particularly outrageous situation, one may—often in behalf of someone else more than for himself—lose all patience and self-control. The harm of such retaliation in kind and such loss of self-possession can probably be overcome. But as a matter of explicit, calculated policy, constructive ends are not served by destructive means. To adopt such means drops the whole conflict to the level set by a bullying oppressor. It scraps the very values purportedly being fought for. Helmut Gollwitzer has written: "We Christians . . . must recognize and proclaim clearly that terror is in fact no protection against terror." [7]

A Respect for Essential Structure

Civil disobedience, under conditions set by Christian faith, ought to indicate a respect for the structure of the community in which it is carried out. That is to say, an act of civil disobedience is not a general uprising questioning the legitimacy of and undertaking the overthrow of the community. While it isolates a specific abuse for dramatic protest, it affirms the community structure in general as the community structure it is prepared to honor and work within. It leaves unquestioned many other essential functions which the government continues to carry out. And it acknowledges its officials—however inept and unworthy their conduct of office may have been—as "the powers that be" who will be held in due respect as long as they are filling the proper functions of their offices. A legal authority put it this way: "The civil disobedient, as such, acts *within* the frame of established authority, not outside it." [8]

It is in this persuasion that disobedients have chosen to break a law, when they must, and accept the appropriate penalty. Those who engage in civil disobedience cannot properly claim a right to such conduct. No state can write laws with the implied qualification: this is the provision of the law, but any citizen is free to disregard it if he feels he must. A legislature, in a pluralistic society, may write compassionate laws which allow for varieties of principled conduct. It may write into some laws "escape hatches"—such as the conscientious objector provision in the Selective Service Act. But a state cannot recognize the justification of civil disobedience. If it did, it would not be a state. The state is not a voluntary association. If it allowed groups to dissociate, it would be "a house divided against itself." A government must determine on laws it believes to be in the general interest and provide the penalties to be assessed for noncompliance. Thus, there may be a moral duty to break the law, but there can be no legal right to do so. Violation of the law must entail an assigned penalty.

Persons engaging in civil disobedience have understood this and have broken laws, prepared to accept the penalties for their action. This practice indicates respect for the structure within which the disobedience takes place, and it also indicates moral seriousness and willingness to undergo personal loss on the part of the persons disobeying the law.

In an earlier chapter some remarks of George F. Kennan were quoted which argued that "Respect for the law is not an obligation which is exhausted or obliterated by willingness to accept the penalty for breaking it." He thinks of this willingness as merely attaching a price tag to an irresponsible act. He compares breaking the law and paying the penalty to paying a quarter at a fair for the chance to break crockery. Given the anguish and suffering which civil disobedients have accepted willingly, Kennan's argument seems not to take the measure of the moral issues at stake—he makes civil disobedience sound almost frivolous. But, more profoundly, he mistakes the intentions of those he opposes. No one agrees to accept the penalty *in order to* break the law. No one feels that his act of lawbreaking is morally justified *because of* his willingness to accept the penalty. One breaks the law because, given his assessment of the law, the situation, and his own duty, he *must* do so. The law is an instrument of evil, and disobedience seems the only honorable course. The penalty follows as the appointed consequence. His act must be judged by asking whether the condition protested was actually as unjust and as unendurable as the disobedient maintained. The one who breaks the law knows in advance that the government cannot be expected to differentiate among the purposes of those who break its laws. The penalty attaches to the disobedient act. Those are the terms on which a person must determine that he is morally bound to violate a law. By accepting those terms, the disobedient citizen affirms the order of the community even while deliberately engaging in opposition to a portion of its stated legislation.*

A Constructive Role in Reordering the Community

Christians who are led in conscience to disobey a law do not terminate their responsible relation to a community once the law has been broken and the penalty paid. Those who encourage and engage in civil disobedience must accept their measure of responsibility in any discreative consequences of acts of disobedience, and they must assist, insofar as they can, in terminating these unwanted effects. Those who have brought a moral problem of a community to an open crisis must, as opportunity allows, work for the healing of the disruption of the community. If there are constructive intentions in their

* Some further discussion of the relation between disobedience and the legal penalty will be found in Appendix III.

action, they must continue by every means possible to have those intentions fulfilled. If acts of civil disobedience have created opportunities for a more just ordering of the community, the disobedients must urge that these opportunities be adequately utilized.

Of course, this constructive role will not always be a possibility. An act of civil disobedience may have accomplished nothing from the point of view of the disobedients, and it may leave them rejected by the community. But civil disobedience is not an end in itself; it is a means, through witness, toward a better community. The means should not so preoccupy the disobedients and those who share their hopes that the constructive intentions with which disobedience was entered upon are forgotten.

THE CONSCIENCE AND THE COMMUNITY

The argument of the previous chapter concluded that civil disobedience is or can be a legitimate calling for a Christian person or group. The thesis that government should always be obeyed has been defended within the Christian community, but such a position would seem to have insuperable difficulties. Given the painful conflicts between authorities which complicate the search for a course of obedience, it seems necessary to recognize that at times a Christian must render to the demands of the state his considered No.

The present chapter would seem to have added that civil disobedience is a perilous calling. Its practice is full of difficulties and uncertainties. Conscientious Christians who agree that civil disobedience is an allowable tactic will yet disagree as to whether or not it was well used in a past instance or as to when and how it might be used in the present. Clarity and agreement are impossible to come by in an issue which, like this one, arises out of a conflict between claims, both of which are legitimate. Further, civil disobedience is a tool which by its very nature calls for unusual wisdom but which by its very nature is likely to attract rash persons (and likely, for that matter, to compel usually restrained persons to act with unchracteristic rashness). Unfortunately, it will often have associated with it a great deal of folly and irrationality. But one can note with gratitude that it also seems to claim more than its share of courage, self-discipline, compassion, sacrifice, and martyrdom.

No question is more common in a discussion of civil disobedience than, "But whose conscience is to determine? Mine?" The risk and peril in civil disobedience make this hesitancy understandable. To go against the collective voice can seem presumptuous. Yet, finally, the answer must be, "Yes, your conscience." Ultimately conscience is individual. To follow it can lead one to desolating isolation even from the communities he most loves and feels most indebted to. Courage to stand alone, if necessary, is required in any issue in which appeal is made to conscience.

In practice, however, a dissenter is seldom in a position of Athanasius against the world. Where ideas disseminate freely, it is unlikely that an opinion on a public matter would be completely unshared. A person who adopts a "far out" position will usually find before long that there are others out there with him.

A course which sets one against the community might well occasion misgivings. Indeed, most persons considering civil disobedience have engaged in rigorous self-questioning. They inquire about their own motives. Am I doing this to bring about beneficial social change, or am I doing it to achieve publicity, self-gratification, or to express my general resentment of authority? What about the probable consequences of my act of public disobedience in the light of all my other responsibilities, and what about its likely effect on those who may use it as an example with inadequate understanding of the issues? If such self-questioning yields a mixed report, that is also the case in all other ethical decisions. Civil disobedience, by its public character, renders more intense the kinds of motives that are the stuff of moral life in general; but little really new is introduced at the personal level. Self-questioning should not induce paralysis. In ambiguous, contingent situations, we, as short-sighted, self-centered persons, must determine and commit ourselves entirely to our duty under God as we see it. There are no other kinds of situations or people.

The private aspect of civil disobedience has perhaps become less prominent than it once was because disobedience is now more characteristically a tool of social protest. But many classic disobedients were, by their acts, disaffiliating from communities which seemed to require their participation in corporate wrong. The individual decided that even if he could not persuade the community to renounce its evil, he could at least refuse to let that evil involve him. A memorable instance is John Woolman's refusal to pay the portion of his taxes which was used in fighting the Indians. (Even more striking, even though no law was involved, was Woolman's practice of paying silver pieces to the slaves when he had stayed at a slave-owning household so that he would not be beneficiary of labor unjustly exacted.) This line of thinking has a certain nobility. It argues in effect: "I cannot be responsible for the community. It will very likely go on doing what it is doing now. But I can at least be responsible for myself. And at the point at which the community would compel me to cooperate in evil, I shall not comply." Even though such motives have (probably since Gandhi) become less central in civil disobedience than the intention to alter the social order, these private considerations remain a significant ethical factor. For many persons, the decision to disobey is a quite individual matter. "I cannot do what the state requires" is the only argument used, and it is sufficient.

The risk in this stance is self-righteousness. No one by his own effort can separate himself from the shortsighted, exploitative community or rid himself of complicity in its unjust acts. Civil disobedience cannot responsibly be undertaken as a device for declaring oneself morally pure while at the same time demonstrating the corruption of the rest of the community. The individual conscience does in a sense transcend the group. It cannot properly allow itself to be dictated by the group, and the group must carefully restrict its effort to coerce it. But a disobedient who supposed his dissent had exempted him from corporate responsibility would have underestimated the subtlety and profundity of the relation between the individual and the group. Civil disobedience is not an occasion for contracting *out* of the community; it is an occasion to adopt a role which (although it may be costly for the disobedient) will be exercised *in* the community and may ultimately be of value *for* the community.

At the most obvious level, civil disobedience is a public act. It is something one does as a citizen, and it is done in the open. Moreover, it is an injection into the community of the kind of force which can gain its point by its drama—its paradoxical mixture of moral claim with apparent illegality. Once such a force has been released publicly, it can bring about unforeseeable and unwanted results. Its drama is likely to attract publicity and misconstruction. Great discretion would seem essential to its effective use. Father Drinan has argued: "Direct action . . . must be proportionate to the injustice sought to be corrected. Massive non-compliance with a law by a substantial number of people cannot be justified unless it is directed towards the correction of a proportionately serious injustice." [9]

These are surely wise words. But they use the language of mathematics. Who is to determine just how much injustice is to be met by how much noncompliance? What measures would apply? Judgments must be made by persons under great pressure, not by mathematicians. Discretion is obviously desirable; it is also impossible to guarantee. The tool of civil disobedience can be discussed realistically only with an awareness that it may be used badly.

One of the factors which will most make a community overlook indiscretion in the carrying out of civil disobedience is the widespread recognition that the action is in a defensible cause. By some commonly accepted large frame of reference, it must be possible to see that the disobedients have a grasp of the great moral realities at the heart of the legal system. They are not using their disobedience of a particular regulation as a way of evading those highest ethical demands to which the community generally consents. Charles Frankel has said: "The goals of those who disobey the law have to lie at the very heart of what we regard as morality before we can say that they have a moral right to do what they are doing." [10]

The rub is that these ultimate moral claims must establish themselves in the conscience of a small, limited, selfish person. A responsible Christian must follow his conscience. He cannot do otherwise. But, in so doing, he must recognize that his conscience is not the voice of God, pure and simple. One's conscience is both informed and dulled by many factors from past experience, and it is subject to self-deception. William Temple once observed:

It is not enough that a man should always do what he thinks to be his duty; there is an even prior duty to that, namely, that he should think to be his duty what really is his duty. All the deepest sins in the nature of most of us are sins that we have not discovered at all. They are very often associated with something about us with which we are particularly well satisfied.[11]

Thus there needs to be some manner of check on the conscience. Always, for a Christian, conscience has reference to a community. One's conscience can be taught and corrected by the fellowship in which one's life is set. The complex relationship between the individual conscience and the community is well summarized by Meyners:

Where resistance is appropriate, it must if possible be undertaken by the Church, by the corporate Christian conscience, or by the largest group conscience achievable within the Church. This will be a partial safeguard against irresponsible radicalism which resists precipitously without adequate justification, without appraising the costs, and with little chance of success. Nevertheless, this corporate conscience on the side of resistance may be rarer than the real need for resistance. The corporate conscience is conservative. Therefore, there must be a place in the fellowship of the Church in which the radical witness of the individual and of small groups are nurtured. These challenge the corporate conscience, activate it to resistance if it ever resists, and sometimes witness directly to society to the will of God where the Church as a whole gives this witness no heed.[12]

Responsible interaction with the community is inescapable—and indeed, can be of great benefit. But in itself it does not simplify decision. Even after an individual has consulted the best insights of others in the Christian fellowship, he still must make his own decision. It may be that he will feel compelled to decide against the counsel of the group. Just as the slower, large community can be the judge of the rash individual, the prophetic individual (or small group) can be judge of the community. This calling is difficult. It requires the strange mixture of humility and boldness which is the characteristic style of confident faith. The individual risks being, by the available standards, irresponsible and a fool—but it will be for Christ's sake.

But the ultimate appeal to Christ is not open to the individual nonconformist only. The uniqueness of the Christian community is that (by profession at least) the final criterion—for each individual conscience and for the communal discourse—is the mind of Christ. It is not just a case of a person in solitude determining what his duty is. Nor is it a case of persons in groups inquiring what their consensus might be. It is a matter of persons speaking on matters of conscience only after all have listened to the Lord of the conscience and of the community. This inward listening is a difficult, life-long task, and one is daily making decisive moral commitments on the basis of a conscience very imperfectly conformed to the mind of Christ.

Hence, any Christian is likely to act foolishly and self-assertively. His moral acts must be an ever-renewed occasion both for repentance and for joy that his confidence is in a God who justifies the sinner and a Christ who, having begun a good work in us, will go on faithfully to complete it. In a sense, every act of Christian civil disobedience is an eschatological act. It represents a break with the age's norms of responsible conduct. But it is done in loyalty to a transcendent reference, and it looks to a final vindication beyond history. It is a bit of judgment on the old and an intrusion of the new apprehended beforehand. The disobedient is not delivered from the ambiguities of historic existence, but in the midst of them he is able to act by faith and to lay claim to the future. Once he is committed to disobedience, he can act spontaneously and gladly. As a man set free, a Christian relaxes and works harder than ever.

Perhaps some indication of response to the mind of Christ can be seen in the broad range of identification with others that the present searching of Christian conscience is calling forth. The American society and the Christian community are alike cut into groups reflecting racial, economic, generational, and cultural divisions. These groups have a great deal of corporate self-consciousness. It is not surprising that blacks and whites, impoverished and affluent, younger and older develop awareness of certain problems and blindness to others. The Christian fellowship is so divided along the same lines as the community and so inclined to see what the community sees and overlook what the community overlooks that its ability to correct the partial views of the persons it reaches is limited. The faith itself becomes adapted to the community so smoothly that it can neither judge nor redeem. But the Lord of all seems

to be declaring himself in the midst of the brokenness of church
and society. Negroes are not required to stand alone on issues
involving their interests. Young persons opposing service in a
war they regard as immoral do not take risks alone. Some
white persons (too often those with little status to imperil, to
be sure) are able to rise above their group interest and stand
alongside their Negro brothers.[13] In a deeply racist society,
the larger claim of man has not been silenced. Some of the
demonstrators, opinion leaders, prisoners, and martyrs on behalf of the Negro have been white. Some of those who are
not themselves under a requirement of military service have
yet taken steps which put them under the same legal jeopardy
as those of military age whose opposition to the war they share.
These gestures of identification and support place one alongside another in risk and calumny. It may, for one companion
in disobedience, be a protest of an outrage felt generally in a
group to which he belongs. For another, it may be a deliberate
act of choice made to associate one who did not have to involve
himself with another who could not avoid involvement. This is
conscientious action in the authentic biblical tradition. One
leaves his comfortable exemption in recognition of a need in
one who is a brother. In compassion, one loses the blindness
and the smugness of his own group and, in some measure,
transcends it. He comes to see his own groups and to see
himself through new eyes. As he divests himself of the limitations of his sense of kind, he draws closer to others, and together they are learning of a Christ whose name may never
be mentioned.

Sometimes in a situation as complex as that of today's
society and in a matter as perilous as civil disobedience, a
Christian person may decide very badly and require and receive with gratitude some correction from others, whether
Christians or not, who were not associated in his folly. However, sometimes he may decide admirably, and he may himself
be a rebuke and a judgment under Christ against those who

should have stood with him in his traitorous trueness but did not. His open disobedience is a reminder that those who obey, no less than those who disobey, are making choices and are under an obligation to act from conscience and consider the morality of their actions.[14] In a varied church acting in a varied society, it seems likely that there will be differing determinations of Christian duty on as controversial a matter as civil disobedience. Some will need to ask forgiveness for doing the things they ought not to have done, and some will need to ask forgiveness for not doing the things they ought to have done.

Civil disobedience would now seem to be a calling for some in the church—for few or for many. But insofar as a civil disobedient specifies that he is acting, in a moral issue, on what he takes to be obedience to one who is his Lord and everyman's Lord, his action requires all to consider freshly the quality of their own obedience. To what extent does that man's No represent what many more should be saying? What I should be saying? Should the No of that Christian rightly be the No of the church? If, on consideration, it seems that at this time it need not, what does the church owe to that disobedient now?

Perhaps the Christian community, in its unity and disagreement, might be thought of as a fellowship of those who, submitting their own consciences to Christ, are determined to retain their bond of acceptance and respect with those who engage equally sincerely in the same process of self-judgment by the same standard and with the same rigor but who yet come out of it with different results.

Edward LeRoy Long recently cited an instance of the way in which this oneness in difference works in action:

In the fall of 1940 a small group of students at Union Theological Seminary in New York refused to register under a newly enacted draft law. Eligible for exemption as theological students—or, declining that, as conscientious objectors—they chose to make an open and public stand against a law they considered morally wrong. The student cabinet, responding to the tension produced within the seminary community by this illegal protest, issued a resolution that said in part:

"On registration day, some of us will register in support of the Selective Service Act. Some will register, taking their stand within the provisions of the act, as conscientious objectors. Some will present to government officials a statement of their inability conscientiously to register under the act.

"We of the student cabinet affirm that, regardless of our disagreements and in some cases of our strong opposition to policies of others, we will hold in respect and reverence those who in sincerity and humility maintain their loyalty to conscience, and will strive through prayer and devotion in the difficult days ahead to maintain in love the community of the Christian faith.[15]

The church, then, in such a spirit, offers to God in Christ all its diverse gifts and callings, trusting that through our conscientious Christian obedience to the state and our equally conscientious Christian disobedience to the state, his will may prevail in his world.

seven

: :

AN EXAMINATION OF
CHRISTIAN NONVIOLENCE

[If you have weapons, take them home; if you do not have them, please do not seek to get them. We cannot solve this problem through retaliatory violence. . . . We must love our white brothers no matter what they do to us. We must make them know that we love them. Jesus still cries out in words that echo across the centuries: "Love your enemies; bless them that curse you; pray for them that despitefully use you." This is what we must live by. We must meet hate with love.[1]

These are words spoken by Martin Luther King, Jr., to a stunned and angry crowd of supporters on a night his home was bombed during the Montgomery, Alabama, bus boycott. They articulate the spirit of nonviolence. Christian civil disobedience has so characteristically used nonviolent action that some examination of this concept and stratagem must be made.

Two initial clarifications may be useful:

1. Christian users of nonviolence often indicate some sense of kinship with the early centuries of the church—the age of persecution and martyrdom. Like the early Christians, these modern counterparts are drawn into a close fellowship of those who suffer at the hands of an uncomprehending community for the sake of Christian conscience. But there is a marked difference between Christians of the two eras. In the early church, the Christians endured suffering patiently because that is all they could do. They protested their innocence of antisocial conduct, and they hoped for a time when the irrational op-

123

position to the very existence of the church might end. But they could not entertain seriously the idea that social structures might change. The modern users of nonviolent protest are protesting things as they are with every expectation that change is possible. If suffering unjustly is a present cost to be borne, it is suffering in a cause which will succeed in altering the purposes and conditions which now seem to determine the general society. The most the early church hoped for was toleration for its own existence. The modern Christian protest intends to influence the community at large.

2. Christian users of nonviolence have also felt some kinship with a tradition of pacifist conscience tracing through Fox and Woolman, Ballou, Thoreau, Tolstoy, and Gandhi. There are certainly aspects of similarity in idea and method among these honored models and between all of them and modern Christian movements; but distinctions must be observed, some of which will be identified in the following pages. Here suffice to note the radical difference between modern nonviolent protest and the doctrine of Tolstoy. Leo Tolstoy thought that he had discovered the real message of Jesus in the passage from the Sermon on the Mount in which Jesus said: "But I say to you, Do not resist one who is evil." [2] Tolstoy was convinced of the necessity of passive nonresistance to evil— especially as that evil was embodied in the oppressive demands of the state. A man of conscience was to meet this powerful evil with even greater strength of character by letting mere force do to him what it would and not engaging in active resistance.[3] Our concern here is not to criticize Tolstoy's understanding of Jesus' ethic but to point out that modern-day Christian nonviolent resistance does not, in fact, bear much resemblance to Tolstoy's teaching. Even though it resembles Tolstoy's position in its refusal to retaliate in kind when force is used, modern Christian nonviolent action, as practiced, is an aggressive tactic. It does not leave evil unopposed. It resists; it carries the challenge to the enemy. It intends that

evil be identified and defied. It means to bring about change. Those against whom a large nonviolent protest is mounted certainly feel its impact as a threat—a powerful force has assumed the initiative. The method may have the look of Tolstoy; the spirit may draw some inspiration from his powerful writing; but the intention is the very opposite of Tolstoy's counsel.

It becomes useful, at this point, to inquire directly what rootage the nonviolent method can rightly claim to have in the Christian gospel.

The situation is far from clear if one wants to trace the actual sources of inspiration of today's users of nonviolence. Martin Luther King acknowledged that he, a Baptist clergyman, received much of the direct inspiration for his work from the successful campaign for Indian independence led by Mahatma Gandhi, a Hindu who explicitly rejected Christianity.[4] Thus the modern movement among Christians is in part indebted to Hindu doctrines. Indeed, the very term "nonviolence" appears to be an English translation of the Sanskrit term *ahimsa* widely used by Gandhi. It means narrowly "abstention," but in the doctrinal background for Gandhi's work it refers more broadly to doing no harm to any living creature.[5] Along with this negative term, Gandhi is associated with the positive term *satyagraha,* usually translated "soul force." It refers to the inner strength of one who does not compromise with oppression but overcomes by enduring all that the oppressor might inflict and emerging still defiant and still determined not to resort to retaliatory violence. These Hindu terms come from a thought world of resignation and belief in the universal oneness of things.

Yet it seems certain that Gandhi's own ideas were shaped in part by Christian influence.[6] Christian ideas (along with other Western political doctrines) influenced Gandhi, and Gandhi's ideas have influenced Christians. The two patterns are mixed, but some disentangling of sources is possible.

The nonviolent resistance which draws on Christian sanctions would have distinctive leading concepts. Evil is not met with nonviolence because it is supposed that evil is weak or that it should not be opposed. Those who practice nonviolence are not naïve about evil; they have had abundant experience of the frightening depth of human hatred and brutality. They know that any eventual unity of all things which Christian faith allows one to hope for is brought about by facing and overcoming the radical disunities of historic existence. Conflict is the normal state of the human community. Groups espousing nonviolence do not exempt themselves from this conflict; they may enter it deeply committed to one side. Indeed, they may heighten the open conflict by their participation. But to the conflict, they bring only one allowable weapon: self-giving love. To meet force with force or hatred with hatred seems sub-Christian. It may bring about the embittered submission of one side to the superior power of another—but that is not reconciliation. To answer force and hate in kind leaves the seeds of further destructive conflict. Self-giving love, by contrast, can diminish the terrible dialectic of force and hate. The pain of conflict can be drawn when one party refuses to retaliate, but instead lets the pain fall on itself and stop there. This is a Christian's calling: to absorb the pain involved in the righting of injustices.

This ethic is, for the Christian, bound up with Jesus as its teacher and exemplar. He proclaimed the kingdom of God—an act of God, initiated in Jesus and his mission. Life in that kingdom had a new quality and was lived on a new basis. Enemies were to be forgiven; good was to be returned for evil. And under the most desolate of circumstances, Jesus practiced his own teaching. At the crucifixion he forgave his own tormentors. He sustained his own dignity and love against opposition and with the usual supports of companionship and understanding withdrawn. A later Christian epistle indicates the place occupied in the imagination of the primitive church by

Jesus' own conduct. The writer encourages his readers to endure suffering by citing Jesus: "When he was reviled, he did not revile in return; when he suffered, he did not threaten" (I Peter 2:23).

But principally for a Christian this ethic is bound up with the gospel itself. That is, nonviolence is not a general ethical principle commended because it is wise or reasonable or because it is more likely to work than is retaliation. Rather, it is a direct derivative of the message of the Cross. As Bonhoeffer once put it, "The cross is the only power in the world which proves that suffering love can avenge and vanquish evil." [7] When God undertook to conquer evil, it was accomplished in the weakness of the Cross. Self-giving love was the only weapon that almighty God himself brought against the "contradiction of sinners."

It is to a share in this redemptive mission that Christ's people are called. "If any man would come after me, let him deny himself, take up his cross, and follow me." A Christian is sustained in his own self-giving ministry, knowing that it is the way of God himself who won strength out of weakness and victory out of defeat. It is because of the Cross that a Christian "glories in his weakness." The paradox of the strength of God made manifest through the weakness of his representative, of the weak things of the world confounding the mighty is basic in the Christian calling. St. Paul counsels that good be returned for evil and that vengeance be left to God. The God who had acted in the Cross and resurrection was man's vindicator; the same God would ultimately be man's vindicator. Meanwhile, the way of the Cross was, for the Christian, the way of freedom, power, and conquest. This was the faith which informed the early Christian use of nonviolence. "The cross is the only justification for the precept of nonviolence, for it alone can kindle a faith in the victory over evil which will enable men to obey that precept." [8]

Thus it seems possible to make a case for nonviolence as

an ethic derivable quite directly from Christian sources. Some pacifists, indeed, would go further and ask that nonviolence be recognized as the only fitting Christian ethic. Any departure from it would seem to be a compromise with the self-assertiveness which is the very heart of sin.

The point is given more force by a consideration of violence. It is apparent to upholders of nonviolence that violence is, by intention, destructive. Violence is not a means taken in hand except to destroy property, community, personhood, or life itself. If nothing is destroyed, violence has not done its appointed work. It is only vindicated by wreckage. Moreover, violence is difficult to control. It is undiscriminating; good is destroyed along with evil. Once violence is introduced, it tends to feed on itself and exceed the intentions of its users. It brings about unwanted results.

More important, violence seems inherently incompatible with self-giving love. It is an extension of self-will. It regards other persons and their ideas and feelings with contempt; it treats them as means. It brutalizes its users as they inflict harm on others. St. Paul once remarked that "Love works no wrong to its neighbor" (Romans 13:10). This seems like a minimal, negative claim to make for Christian love, but it is enough to clarify the irreconcilability of love so described and personal violence in any form.

But the argument is not so simple. Both violence and nonviolence are more ambiguous than the foregoing paragraphs have indicated.

It is difficult to argue that violence is always and everywhere intrinsically evil. An example may be useful: Two men are struggling. The fight is desperate and evenly matched. But one is an attacker; the other is defending himself and his terrified wife. Both are using violence. But certainly the moral quality represented by the two men is not for that reason comparable.[9] In other words, the use of physical force need not in itself obscure or prejudge all moral distinctions.

The ambiguity here may be in the range of meaning which

can be covered by the word "violence." If the reference is to uncontrolled, destructive action, the term "violence" has a negative moral sense inevitably. But if the reference is just to strong force, the term "violence" need not be negative. Perhaps it would be best to clarify by a simple decision to use words in a specific way. "Violence" might be used for the negative meanings and "force" for the neutral or positive meanings. So used, "force" might be considered a restraint—to be used no more than required—against violence. Many persons who are not absolute pacifists would welcome some such distinction which would give them a word other than "violence" to designate the kinds of physical force which they would regard as justifiable. But words seem to mean what custom makes them mean, and the ambiguity in the term "violence" will doubtless persist.

Even if terminology were clarified, violence—violence of the starkest sort—would continue to have a mixed record. The ambiguity and unpredictability of human affairs is such that violence, even violence undertaken in bad causes, can be productive of some good. This observation may not be a tribute to violence itself so much as to the resilience of the human spirit which is able to affirm itself in the midst of ruin. Nevertheless, new conditions of genuine benefit to some persons can result from the employment of immoderate and harsh force.

If, moreover, it is urged that violence is destructive, it might be replied that there are some things which ought to be destroyed. Can anyone seriously argue that Hitler's gas ovens ought not to have been sabotaged? Things which, either in their actual use or as symbols, represent man's tyranny over, or his exploitation or brutalization of, his brothers might well become targets for destructive acts. Such acts would no doubt be violent. But if the focus of the act is significant enough and if personal injury is avoided, such destruction might not be merely understandable, it might be morally defensible.

Further, some persons who have a categorical fear of

violence and its effect in society fail to realize that violence
is present now in the social order. Violence, more or less continuous, is the normal state of the American community—
perhaps of civilized man. Hannah Arendt has commented:

> Cain slew Abel, and Romulus slew Remus; violence was the
> beginning and, by the same token, no beginning could be made with-
> out using violence, without violating. The first recorded deeds in
> our biblical and our secular tradition, whether known to be legend-
> ary or believed in as historical fact, have traveled through the cen-
> turies with the force which human thought achieves in the rare in-
> stances when it produces cogent metaphors or universally applicable
> tales. The tale spoke clearly: whatever brotherhood human beings
> may be capable of has grown out of fratricide, whatever political
> organization men have achieved has its origin in crime.[10]

Violence is regularly employed by the strong against the
weak in such areas as economic repression, the use of police
power to support the already privileged, the psychological
violence which intimidates the downtrodden. Violence is present, and a great many people—possibly in most cases unaware
of the fact—benefit by it. It is customary to hear those in
advantaged position in the society announce their horror of
violence. It might be ventured that persons in the favored
groups do not really fear the introduction of violence into society; it is already there. They fear its adoption by its victims
against their oppressors. The only basis on which a person
is entitled to oppose violence which may be used in altering
an unjust social status is his consistent opposition to the use of
violence in the maintenance of that status.

Thus, surprisingly perhaps, there are points to be considered which can lend some moral stature to violence, or at
least render understandable the processes which employ it in
the community. Violence is not in all circumstances an unqualified evil.

Given this ambiguity of the moral quality of violence,

perhaps some limitations on the method of nonviolence may be suggested:

The tactic of nonviolence cannot become a policy for nations or for many other institutional units. Human societies are gathered around certain collective self-interests in such a way as to have only a restricted ability to rise altruistically above themselves. They exist because of something they have to defend. Their conduct as collectivities can often be restrained and generous. But they are unlikely voluntarily to restrict their own power or reduce their own status. Under threat they are unlikely to limit the manner of their self-defense in such a way as to jeopardize their own survival. Situations in which they are compelled to use force may be part of their very existence. Consistent nonviolence might be suicide.

The tactic of nonviolence depends for its effectiveness on the presence of human sensitivity in the opponent. It appeals to the conscience of the oppressor and assumes his general consent to the justice of the cause of the oppressed. Where the oppressor is utterly cynical, nonviolence probably only confirms him in his inhumanity. Where there is no recognition of the justice of the nonviolent party, nonviolence will be unlikely to produce change. In situations like the English colonial rule in India or the churchgoing, Declaration of Independence-quoting American south, nonviolent protest can be highly effective. The oppressor's bad conscience is an ally.

In situations like the Third Reich in Germany, nonviolent resistance was unable to effect change. It simply led to the destruction of the resisters and confirmed the Nazi doctrine of the inferiority of these passive groups.

Success in nonviolent protest also depends on certain psychological conditions which are not everywhere present. Dr. Kenneth Clark observes that nonviolent demonstrations in behalf of Negroes have been effective, "but they must inevitably decrease in impact. Intense and dramatic experiences are subject to the psychological law of diminishing returns—a decrease in sensitivity both on the part of the participant and the audience." [11] Nonviolent protest which is initially successful is likely to become less so if the method is used repeatedly and consistently. When the method begins to fail in getting results, its adherents (unless carried by strong moral resource) may feel betrayed, and in disillusionment they may repudiate all moderation.

Of course, some upholders of nonviolence would maintain that no consideration should be given to questions of success or effectiveness. The demands on a Christian that he not acquiesce in evil and that he not resort to violence in opposing it are held to be absolute. He must abide by them regardless of apparent failure. This, it is held, is the way of the Cross—an uncalculating self-sacrifice.

This spirit, to be sure, has inspired much Christian heroism in the past. Persons have accepted abuse, hatred, and martyrdom without resort to retaliation. Gentle, peace-loving groups have met endless harassment, legal disability, and outright attack with serenity and dignity. Consistent nonviolence informed by the highest Christian dedication carries no guarantee that it will prevail—in the short or the long run. It may go down in unremembered defeat. Yet there are those who will feel bound to the principle no matter what the circumstances or the expectation.

This attitude may be thoroughly admirable. In situations in which choice is quite limited, if all one can do is to endure his lot bravely to the end, it is important that he do exactly that. But in modern American society, mobility, while limited, is still possible. Change still takes place. Oppressed groups can assume some initiative and challenge the social pattern. They have some choice of method. The nonviolent demonstration is valuable insofar as it works. The question of results is not illegitimate. A Christian is a follower of Jesus Christ, not Don Quixote. The aim is change. As long as channels are open for doing so, the hope of socially committed Christians ought to be to bring about without violence the sort of redress of injustice which might otherwise be attempted by force—with even greater waste and destructiveness. In other words, a transfer or enlargement of political power is perhaps the moral equivalent of violent revolution. Hence, if the wise use of nonviolent demonstrations brings such change about, it is a means worth using. But if this means has limitations and if there are other means which will achieve the same effect, the initiative of those Christian persons seeking a better community is not bound to that one style of action.

All of this is to say that the church ought to value nonviolent action and use it (and join with others who use it) for good ends, but the church should not absolutize it. Nonviolence does have limitations; it is only one among viable Christian stratagems for community action in our time.

However, when it is used, nonviolent action is a stratagem with great strengths. Four of these might be itemized here:

First, it takes seriously the means to be used to accomplish humane ends. By the analysis of those using nonviolence, violence, force, compulsion are means unsuited to the production of a better social order. Violence destroys and is thereby contrary to a constructive intention. Physical force secures its way by threat or the access to visibly superior power; hence it is a means out of harmony with the free consent which must be part of a lasting commitment of the community to larger purposes. If one's aim is simply to replace one dominant, oppressing group with another composed of the former victims of the old regime, questions of means are of no importance. Anything that works to break the power of the old group and bring about its downfall is acceptable. No means used can be regarded as corrupting the user, as long as the user represents the new group which takes its own cause to be so inherently right as to justify anything done to secure its success. But if the aim is justice for all and the reconciliation of all groups in a richer, more comprehensive unity, means cannot be ignored.

The nonviolent tactic seeks to use human means with human beings. It seeks to use just means in its search for larger justice. It seeks to employ peaceful means to secure peace.

This rigorous concern for the use of means in keeping with a Christian end gives depth to the nonviolent ethic. It is penetrating and self-critical, not naïve. Gains made with due attention to fit means may carry less bitterness into the new synthesis. The process of change is less likely to be beguiled into the overreactions in which many ill-considered actions have to be undone later.

Second, nonviolent action requires great moral discipline. Persons determine to challenge social evil, letting the pain of the challenge and readjustment fall on themselves. They determine to manifest—under any provocation—only self-giving love. This course requires extraordinary self-discipline. It expects a sustained hatred of community injustice but at the same time it disallows the normal ways in which such hatred would be expressed.[12]

The demonstrations which have been effective have often used training sessions in nonviolent technique. Young people have drilled one another in how to respond to abusive language and how to keep their composure under outright attack. Negroes and their sympathizers have sat-in at segregated lunch counters and had verbal abuse heaped on them, salt, pepper, mustard, and catsup poured on them, and had blows and burns from lighted cigarettes administered by the flower of local youth standing around. But they have borne it with dignity and have not retaliated. This discipline—essential to the success of nonviolent action—represents moral courage and restraint of a very high order.

Perhaps the demands of the nonviolent method are so great that it cannot be used successfully by large numbers of people over a long period of time. A strong sense of dedication—renewed by whatever for a given person is his own ultimate religious sanction—is necessary to keep alive a calling which rechannels self-assertion into such uncongenial forms. Quite possibly the combination of social protest and the denial of violence as a means for that protest is an unstable mixture. The protest may revert to the use of force; the age-old method of retaliation may reassert itself. But while the discipline lasts (and there is no inherent reason why, among select persons with a sense of calling, it may not last for generations) it demonstrates an alternative to the terrible dialectic of an eye for an eye, the end of which is universal blindness.

Third, the nonviolent method respects the opponent. It sees him as a man and credits him with a conscience. The community injustice or immorality which is being protested by nonviolent action is represented by structures which the protesting group is determined to alter or bring down. But those structures are always identified with persons who are their custodians. Violence used in attacking the detested community structure tends to fall as harm inflicted on persons who are not detested. Persons who blindly defend social injustice are usually victims of widespread prejudice which has over a lifetime allowed them no alternative. They are to be understood and loved even while the kind of community they defend is being attacked. It is hoped that these persons would be able to live more happily and fully in a freer and more just community. Hence change must be brought about in such a way as to show brotherly concern for all who must live together in a refashioned community.

Nonviolence is not felt by community officials against whom it is used as a tactic concerned about their well-being. They will usually feel deeply threatened by it. They can be provoked, by their own misgivings about their proper response, into taking crude and excessive measures with docile, explicitly nonresisting people. A jail full of irrepressibly confident persons who pray for their captors can be an intimidating experience for a sheriff or police officer.

But the opposite also happens. Practitioners of nonviolence sometimes speak of "moral jiu-jitsu." A person accustomed to using force expects to be met by resentment and counterforce. When he is not, he is taken by surprise and thrown off balance.[13]

The impact on the opponent sought by nonviolent action is not, however, a short-term tactical advantage. The nonviolent method puts an appeal to the opponent's conscience. It inflicts no harm and stands ready to absorb an indefinite amount. This stratagem in effect says to an opponent: "You are a humane person—probably a decent family man and a responsible employee. You are here trying to do your job, and you are quite threatened by this challenge to expected community norms. But you can recognize the rightness of our claim to a hearing and to being allowed the exercise of common humanity—even if that recognition is mixed with many other feelings about us and our intentions. Since we use no violence, you will get tired of your role before long. Your arm will get tired of hitting us. But, more important, your conscience will get tired of your continuing to inflict pain on unresisting persons. Our secret weapon is your unacknowledged recognition of us as fellow human beings." This crediting of one's opponent with a conscience is a judgment made without, in all cases, any supporting evidence. The actions of bullying officialdom encouraged by a hate-driven community can render the bonds with human feeling and conduct very tenuous. (Widespread indignation outside a local area can sometimes moderate the actions of the oppressor and support the nonviolent protester.) In most cases, however, the use of nonviolence is recognized—even by its direct targets—as a means calculated to keep humanity intact on both sides of community conflict. If it is illusory to expect that nonviolent protest will, in the end, win over one's opponent, at least it is not a means which will make that conversion impossible.

Fourth, nonviolence affirms the structure of the community. The restraint used in nonviolent action is hardly the method for a revolutionary intention. Anyone using nonviolence obviously means to mount his protest within the terms of the existing community, expecting that the necessary self-correction can be made and the community left intact. These laws, these enforcement officers, these judges are regarded as having the rights over one's person pertaining to their place in the community. A protester will disobey the law and pay the set penalty; the policeman will arrest; the judge will sentence. Everyone does his quite regular, appointed duty. Moral dissent is registered, and if change is to be the result, suffering will not have been inflicted on others by those initiating the protest.

It might be noted that the two courses, nonviolent protest and incipient revolution, are readily confused. Since a great deal more revolution is talked about and attempted unsuccessfully than is brought off, much early revolutionary effort and theory looks and sounds like civil disobedience. Perhaps even those involved could not always say of which mind they are. But Christian nonviolent action as we have known it in this country is not rebellion. It accepts the basic terms of life within a political order and of *my* life within *this* political order. It sets about the correction of politically caused misery by the change of political structures.

This discussion will have suggested that there is a great deal to be said both theoretically and practically for nonviolent action. Its adoption by the protesting forces of the Christian community is natural.

However, in a complex world, it would be unwise for the Christian community to absolutize its alliance with nonviolence. Most contemporary discussion as well as most use of the method has grown from within the Christian community of the democratic countries of the West. It has been an essentially middle-class product of the thinking and style of middle-class churches. It has come to prominence at a time of internal stress and international tension. What might be best in this situation cannot determine what might be best in other places or under other circumstances. Extreme situations alter the sense of Christian duty quite radically. Dietrich Bonhoeffer, for example, as a young man was inclined toward pacifism. Yet, on his final return to Germany, he (with others) became convinced that the Hitler regime was so evil and so unopposable by political methods that the line of Christian duty lay in resistance and finally in the determination to eliminate Hitler.[14] This was an agonizing reversal of direction for Bonhoeffer. The integrity of the process by which he came to this conclusion indicates that the Christian mind on the use of violence might be of more than one opinion. Extreme situations such as Nazi Germany should not establish precedents to be lightly adopted elsewhere. But neither should patterns drawn up for flexible societies responsive to moral appeal be assumed to be universally applicable. The absolute Christian calling is to obedience, but the form of that obedience is relative to a specific situation and the opportunities and limitations it presents.

But, with these qualifications recognized, nonviolent protest is a valuable weapon in the offensive armament of the Christian community. Some of its critics see nothing but the community disruption which is sometimes associated with it. It strikes them as being of the same spirit as the irresponsible rioting and destruction which mar our times. The pictures of the two kinds of events which appear in the mass media show confrontations with police, disorder, and arrests; they look alike. But it is certainly a strange kind of blindness which cannot differentiate between, on the one hand, open riot born out of hatred, despair, and nihilism and, on the other hand, responsible protest aimed at relieving some of the causes of the despair and hatred. One is smallpox, ugly and virulent. The other is cowpox, administered by a physician as a preventive. It does bring on a slight rash, but this effect is temporary. The medication is health-bringing in the long run. Despite the opposition of bigots and the uncomprehending abuse of a threatened establishment, a small group of courageous persons carrying on nonviolent protest against grave inequities and getting some results may for a decade have stood between American society and holocaust.

eight

: :

REVOLUTION
AND OBEDIENCE

There is an old Chinese curse which goes: "May you live in interesting times." [1] The curse has fallen on this generation. A few years ago, our times were spoken of as an "era of rapid social change." The phrase seemed adequate to suggest the widespread, accelerated stir of events. But now it seems almost a euphemism. Changes of a more radical nature are taking place— and at an even more rapid pace. Another phrase is required. Our times are now widely described as an "era of revolution." [2]

The term is evocative. It speaks of old models and forms being challenged and replaced with something new and different. It suggests that such change is often a process filled with conflict, resistance, and tension; the changes are often brought about abruptly and with inevitable pain and waste. But the term "revolution" has now been applied to such varied kinds of change that it has lost definiteness. Sharp shifts in ideas, tastes, customs —or even technology—are spoken of as "revolutions." (It is possible to hear of the "computer revolution" or the "hi-fi revolution.") Moreover, the term is applied to the determination of groups which have been excluded from economic and political power to claim their rightful place in society—even though such a movement may draw on the oldest and most basic of the commitments of the society as a whole. (Thus, the "civil rights revolution" or the "Negro revolution." When humane, liberal ideals have been ignored, it becomes "revolutionary" to insist that they be taken seriously. The application of the term "revo-

139

lution" to these various areas of life is an index of a pervasive mood of our time. But as long as changes in such things as taste, ideas, ways of life, or even distribution of wealth and power are carried out within the established political order (using its processes, respecting its structure, and drawing on its informing ideals), they are "revolutions" only in a somewhat derivative or metaphorical sense of the term. The most stunning changes, if they leave the political order substantially intact, are not "revolution" in the most specific, historical sense.

In the most basic sense, the term "revolution" has denoted a political act intended to restructure the political order and to replace those who bear authority within it. In view of the "hidden violence" by which authorities maintain themselves in power, it is seldom possible to dislodge incumbent forces without resort to overt violence. The expression "era of revolution" used of the present period in history must include this explosive, political sense of the word "revolution." In many parts of the world, critics are voicing disillusion with conventionally ordered society and its possibilities of self-correction. Their critique of the soul and style of existing communities is so radical that willing response seems improbable. In some cases, the target is a state in which a reactionary aristocracy (often with its captive religion to lend it authority) has oppressed great masses of people. In other cases, the target is a reactionary middle-class society (with its captive religion) which seems insensitive and complacent in the face of appalling inequity. In either case, the critics regard existing systems as having forfeited their claim to the loyalty of moral persons. The only obligation open to persons of integrity, as these critics see it, is to work in whatever ways are open to them toward the collapse of systems which are corrupt and discredited. Only revolution and a radical reordering of society can undo wrongs so immense and so resistant to change. Such revolutionists would ask: How can one work for radical change within the established ground rules of the political community when those ground rules are themselves part of the problem?

Those ground rules seem to be a tool used by a dominant group to maintain itself in its advantaged position.

Those persons or groups which see things this way and commit themselves to revolution require special discussion in a general review of civil disobedience, for they too will engage in deliberate, conscientious lawbreaking. But their violations of civil laws are intended as steps in bringing existing political structures down. Even when they lack the power to be a serious threat to established government, their conduct toward the law will be that of revolutionaries.

IN BEHALF OF REVOLUTION

As such ideas are heard with greater frequency and insistence in our society, they are met with outright, vehement rejection by a great many (probably, indeed, by most) persons. American society has been generous to most of its people; they have a great deal that they want to preserve. They have a stake in the existing system. It is all but impossible for them to comprehend the style of those who (in the American setting or any other) are dedicated to revolution.

It is not the purpose of this chapter to justify or to condemn any specific revolution or revolutionary doctrine, past or present. But if some sympathy for and understanding of the revolutionary use of civil disobedience is to be established, it is probably necessary to observe that revolutions have been justified by responsible authorities, and their results have been accepted gratefully by very many persons in the modern world.

A primary instance is, of course, the United States. Hannah Arendt comments on the persistent "failure to remember that a revolution gave birth to the United States and that the republic was brought into existence by no 'historical necessity' and no organic development, but by a deliberate act: the foundation of freedom." [3] The "deliberate act" was undertaken by highly articulate men. They worked out their case over several decades in an extensive literature, and they presented it to the world compellingly:

> We hold these truths to be self-evident, that all men are created equal, that they are endowed by their Creator with certain un-alienable Rights, that among these are Life, Liberty and the pursuit of Happiness.—That to secure these rights, Governments are instituted among Men, deriving their just powers from the consent of the governed,—That whenever any Form of Government becomes destructive of these ends, it is the Right of the People to alter or to abolish it, and to institute new Government, laying its foundation on such principles and organizing its powers in such form, as to them shall seem most likely to effect their Safety and Happiness. Prudence, indeed, will dictate that Governments long established should not be changed for light and transient causes; and accordingly all experience hath shown, that mankind are more disposed to suffer, while evils are sufferable, than to right themselves by abolishing the forms to which they are accustomed. But when a long train of abuses and usurpations, pursuing invariably the same Object evinces a design to reduce them under absolute Despotism, it is their right, it is their duty to throw off such Government, and to provide new Guards for their future security.[4]

This is probably the classic statement of the matter in political terms. It remains a powerful formulation and radical in its implications even after nearly two hundred years.

Many persons in the modern community will not care particularly that the theological tradition can also be cited in defense of revolution; the theology will not seem to them to add anything. But thoughtful members of the Christian fellowship must, for their part, seek to relate their political doctrines to their ultimate faith commitment and the discourse which surrounds and explicates it. A direct relation between revolution and classic Christian ethics was stated by the German theologian (and lover of order) Emil Brunner. He wrote:

> The existing orders, behind which stands the Divine order, constitute the framework within which our service of our neighbor is

to be performed; they form the vessel which we are to fill with the content of love. . . . But there are vessels which are contrary to this content of love, and it is quite possible that such vessels ought to be smashed. Where the existing order is no longer useful but harmful, it is ripe for destruction. . . .

In principle revolution stands upon exactly the same footing as that of obedience of the subject to his superior authority. . . . Revolution can only be allowed . . . as a necessary transition to a new order; but, as such, under certain circumstances, as an unavoidable process of transition, revolution is certainly justified.[5]

But neither Brunner nor any other ethicist until quite recently did much to develop an idea of revolution related to the theological tradition. If a divided church, deeply immersed in its society at a time calling for decisiveness, is to be able to discern and respond to the purposes of the living God, more theological effort is required. Harvey Cox has called for "a theology of social change." He explains: "We are trying to live in a period of revolution without a theology of revolution. The development of such a theology should be the first item on the theological agenda today." [6]

Others have the same sense of priorities, and a small but flourishing literature now exists on "a theology of revolution," and in certain portions of the church few topics are more widely discussed. It seems that the crisis of revolutionary times cannot only elicit fresh political ideas and forces, it can also bring neglected aspects of the Christian message and mission to self-consciousness. The God of Christian theology is not only the God in whose order the orders of man are established, he is the God by whose order the disorders of man are judged. The biblical story has a recurring motif of the divine inversion of human ordering and expectation. God acts to overturn thrones, nations, and empires. He puts down the mighty from their seat and exalts the humble and meek. He calls weak things of the world to confound the mighty. The apocalyptic literature anticipates a great reversal of stations in the final kingdom.[7] This "inverting motif" is widely disregarded when society is relatively stable and the church relatively comfortable; it can be too upsetting a doctrine. But in revolutionary eras, it is rediscovered. The radical social implications of the gospel are once again articulated. Persons who are in touch with the biblical story recognize a familiar hand in the social forces which are calling the disinherited to challenge the privileged, the poor of the world to confound the rich, and the black things of the world to confound the white.

When Christians are called upon to live in revolutionary times, they, as Christian believers (no less than as citizens), are participants in, and interpreters and critics of, the revolutionary forces. Life seems intensified in the revolutionary judgment which falls on the old and the coming to birth of the new. Once again "the time is fulfilled." An alert Christian feels himself close to the crisis of the kingdom as brought by Christ and as pledged in final judgment. He is strangely at home in such times, for he belongs to a fellowship which was born out of a cross and a resurrection. His own deepest commitments are drawn out by fresh and hopeful political possibilities and by a new awareness of aspects of his own gospel.

THE ALTERATION OF GUIDELINES

Chapter Six of this book suggested some guidelines intended to help Christian disobedience to be more, rather than less, responsible. These guidelines apply to civil disobedience which is carried out in general confidence in the political structure. Observing these classic restraints, one breaks a law (when he must) to demonstrate a specific evil, expecting that remedial steps can and will be taken. Certainly the greater part of the civil disobedience by which American society has been challenged in the past and with which it must reckon now is of this type. It draws on the ideals and purposes which have informed the ordered community, and it intends to be supportive of that community. It is meant to incite the community's own better mind to reassert itself. For such disobedience, the discussion of the earlier chapter would apply.

But civil disobedience undertaken as part of revolution is a different thing. Such disobedience is an attack on established structures; it intends to contribute to their destruction. The moral controls of such disobedience are different. Special discussion must be devoted to disobedience in revolution.

A very large factor in the situation is altered by the revolutionary intention. The disobedience discussed in previous chapters worked within the structures of the community and demonstrated general loyalty to them. Many of the rules of self-discipline which disobedients with such intentions would set for themselves would grow out of that positive relation to the structured community. But in revolution, the whole attitude toward the existing state is altered—and much of the pattern of responsible disobedience is altered as a consequence. Those intending revolution will already have determined that, in their view, the existing state constitutes a very great evil. Moral judgments and priorities will then be seen with primary reference to that determination. Having decided that the established system is so defective that it must be brought down, the revolutionist will consider as good such actions as will contribute to this downfall. Matters of timing and tactics might necessitate restraint—a specific act of defiance might seem unwise or self-defeating at a given moment. But, in a revolutionary situation, the aim would not be, in the ordinary sense, to choose the lesser of evils, but to inflict maximum damage on the system in power—and, of course, to remain strong and free to strike again.

Similarly, civil disobedience intending to work within established structures would be used only as a last resort, but in revolution it would not. Disobedience will be engaged in whenever it might further the intentions of the revolutionaries. It might be among the first of their overt actions. Since the overthrow of the system itself is the order of the day, they will not explore constitutional avenues of change before resorting to disobedience. (Presumably, however, revolution would not itself be entered upon except after a long and frustrating experience of the reluctance of the existing system to reform itself. The Founding Fathers claimed that they had borne much patiently, but that the time for patience had come to an end—"Our repeated Petitions have been answered only by repeated injury.")

In the earlier chapter, it was pointed out that civil disobedience undertaken within the existing political structures focuses its protest on specific abuses. By contrast, disobedience which is part of revolt would usually feel under no similar necessity to identify specific aims. It sees the concrete abuses of the society as symptoms of disease pervading the system generally. Though it may be deemed in the interest of rebels to dramatize particular injustices in the existing system in order to win popular support for radical dissent and alienate support from the government, there is no recognition of an absolute necessity to do so. The ultimate aim in revolution is not the correction of this or that abuse but the overthrow of the prevailing system as a whole. Civil disobedience which embarrassed the government or seriously interfered with its ability to govern might be considered compatible with the revolutionary intent. In such a situation, disobedience would be used only as a gesture of general defiance.

The change of explicit aims with which disobedience is undertaken might similarly require a restatement of appropriate means. Neither in protest within an existing system nor in revolution can the end be used to justify any means whatever. Such things as self-restraint and the avoidance of harm to innocent persons are always implied in a moral intent—though they are often difficult to secure. It is doubtless possible to win some revolutions by nonviolent means. An extremely unpopular regime, for example, might be made to topple by widespread, passive noncompliance. But when an oppressive government is maintained in power by a brutal and unscrupulous use of force and fear, it is necessary for revolutionaries to mount their opposition realistically. Revolutionary forces must have the necessary strength and weapons to accomplish their aims and the determination to use them. Restraint or scruples or incompetence which prevent victory may be difficult to assess historically. (Participants in the "officers' plot" against Hitler are remembered with honor now. They were high-minded men committed to a difficult venture, and they were willing to take the required risks and employ the necessary means. But they failed, and their heroic effort did very little good. Hitler survived, and all of the participants in the plot were savagely executed.) When the regime in power is itself a monstrous crime, it may require violent and deceitful means to overthrow it—yet such means may be vindicated in "the Opinions of mankind."

The conditions for civil disobedience cited earlier included the traditional thesis that civil disobedients accept the penalty for their lawbreaking. But a revolutionary situation changes that condition, too. Those who break laws as part of a rebellion feel little obligation to accept the legal penalty for their acts. In a situation of limited civil disobedience, the penalty is accepted as a gesture of assent to the order of the community, but that order is the very thing that a revolutionist has rejected. He will feel that little respect is due it. Moreover, quite practically, a revolutionist in prison is of no further use to the revolution—unless it is possible to turn his imprisonment (or even his martyrdom) into an asset. Persons intent on revolution simply break the law and avoid apprehension (unless dramatic arrest and jailing seems to offer advantages to their cause). They consider it important to remain free to fight another day.

It will be apparent from this brief survey of the modification —indeed, in some cases the virtual reversal—of the normal guidelines governing civil disobedience that revolution creates a morally abnormal, anomalous, paradoxical situation. Political order is a very important bond in a society. Within that order, human dignity is understood and respected, values and priorities are accepted, normal expectations for behavior are understood, mutual trust is expected, and mutual responsibilities are enforced. When that political order itself becomes deeply corrupted, the moral world within which citizens live becomes confused. Human worth and common values are now uncertain. Behavior that could be considered responsible in the normal situation may be too complacent at such a crisis; and behavior considered terribly irresponsible in that situation may now become defensible—if not actually required—given the grossly unjust political order. Revolution is thus carried out in a morally shaken world. But one should not on that account use revolution as a release from responsible action and rigorous ethical thought and say "anything goes." In times of crisis one must think harder than ever and be tested more deeply than ever. The risks of deciding unwisely are increased—but so are the possibilities of taking more fully human, significant actions. But in the strangeness of a revolutionary situation, one must think and act without the support of the customary ground rules of community acting in the customary way.

DISTINCTIONS AND CONFUSIONS

The foregoing discussion will have suggested that civil disobedience can be carried out in two distinguishable styles and with two distinguishable intentions. There is one circle of means and ends which supports the essential structure of the community and another which attacks it. It might be hoped that those engaged in civil disobedience would be able to recognize this distinction and act accordingly. If they intend to disobey while respecting essential community order, they ought to accept the limitations and discipline of classic civil disobedience. They ought to realize that if they step into another style of disobedience and throw off the classic restraints, they are actually within the circle of the ends and means of revolutionists. Revolution—with its peril and cost—may be what is wanted. But the decision to enter on this course ought to be quite deliberate and undertaken in awareness of what may be involved. One ought not to slip into being a revolutionary through inadvertence.

Similarly, it might be hoped that this distinction between two styles and intentions would be clear to those authorities who must respond to civil disobedience and defend public order. The government and public opinion ought to sense the restraint and the constructive intent of classic disobedience. Even though punishment for law violations may be thought necessary, authorities might be expected to recognize the disobedients as allies working within the essential structure for a better society. But revolutionists, by contrast, have mounted a direct challenge to the government. One of the functions of government is to provide for "domestic tranquility." No government can acquiesce in its own overthrow or consent to the reduction of order to chaos. The government is bound to defend its right and its ability to govern. While the freedoms of speech, assembly, press, and petition must be preserved, active steps toward the overthrow of the appointed order must be repressed. Gently or brutally, rightly or wrongly, the state must, by definition and necessity, protect itself.

Doubtless some distinction along these lines would be widely recognized and observed if human life were tidy and social processes were rational. But in experience this clarity is not always found. Ethical analysis must deal with what is, not impose its notion of what ought to be. Some disobedients have, of course, articulated their purposes and controlled their methods quite consistently along the lines referred to here as "classic disobedience" described in Chapters Five and Six of this book and exemplified in Thoreau, Gandhi, and King). Some revolutionists have declared their intentions in manifestoes and have been unambiguous from the start. But there is abundant occasion in practice for this distinction to become lost.

Persons who begin a course of civil disobedience motivated by innocent idealism and intending only to work within their political system for the correction of significant abuses may, in the process of encounter with uncomprehending and unyielding official opposition, find themselves on a far more radical course. They may be driven to a more fundamental critique of the existing order and moved sharply toward revolution. At any moment in this process, the conscious mind of the protesters may run out ahead of or lag behind their actual commitments; they may not know in which of these circles they mean to locate themselves. If frustration in securing even limited results has led to a revolutionary stance, the unexpected accomplishment of important gains can restore some faith in the adaptability of the system and reduce the pressure for its total overthrow.

Confusion about intention seems to increase when revolution (more or less defined) attains some popularity. In our time, revolutionary and anarchistic talk is abundant and cheap. Revolutionary theory is widely discussed; revolutionary figures are heroes to many. Enough groups feel enough alienation from the society at large so that such talk has a ready audience—even among some persons who are probably not prepared to act on its implications. The dedicated revolutionaries are apparently few, but they can command fairly wide sympathy. Articulate revolutionism becomes a useful stance through which persons can express their profound rejection of things as they are. How much of it is meant really seriously and how much of it is little more than a game would only become known in a kind of testing such as has not yet been attempted.

The distinction between the two styles and aims is further confused by the likelihood that many of those who work for revolution find it in their interest to conceal that intention. Persons undertaking the overthrow of an existing regime will not scruple against the use of deliberate deception. Words are tools of revolution, and if destructive acts can be veiled in accepted pieties with some tactical advantage, such misleading representation of their purposes will be made.

It is not only possible for the forces of dissent to misunderstand or deliberately to misstate their own cause, it is also likely that, for their part, governmental authorities under attack will put the worst possible construction on the words and acts of dissenters. Most governments show a tendency to identify their own good with the very basis and continuance of society. Governments—especially those which are insecure or defensive—will have difficulty in distinguishing between loyal disobedience and outright rebellion. All opposition will tend, from the official point of view, to look like revolution and to constitute a fundamental threat. The power of the state to punish and to intimidate will then be used to stop open dissent. The government's influence over communication media will be used to hold dissenters up to ridicule and keep their case from being heard on its own terms.

In sum, the distinction which has been made throughout this book between civil disobedience carried out within the essential structures of society and outright revolt is a useful distinction, a distinction under which certain forces of dissent and disobedience clearly fall to one side or to the other—but a distinction which does not always fare well in practice. It cannot be used without recognizing its limitations. Some persons who intend only loyal disobedience can use the rhetoric of revolution and be pushed thereby in a more radical direction. Some dissenters, at some moments at least, may be so ambivalent in their loyalties that the application of the categories of this distinction to their thought and actions cannot be made without falsifying the real situation. Some persons intent on actual revolt will not say so. Government, in many instances, does not recognize the point of this distinction—even though their own task as well as the peace of the society might be helped by such a recognition.

These forces are worth mention here—and not just because they confuse the distinction which we have been making. Such ambivalent factors are among the important forces that polarize a society and set groups in such radical opposition to one another that reconciliation is neither possible nor wanted. When common ground in trust or in definition of terms or values is lost, there is an escalation of rhetoric on both sides. Neither the professional revolutionary nor the intransigent government can or will concede anything. The one seeks revolution rather than specific reforms, and feels no need to speak or act in good faith toward the state. The other reacts by heavy-handed, undiscriminating defense of established powers. The quiet voice and persistent pressure of classic, nonviolent civil disobedience acting within the existing order is then lost in the tension between these extreme positions.

SOME ESSENTIAL CAUTIONS

For the most part, the argument in this chapter thus far has dealt with revolution against oppression—revolution which can in some sense be justified. Since revolution is an uncongenial thing for the greater part of middle-class American society, the discussion here has tried to show grounds on which there might be responsible sympathy for revolt. It has been argued that this positive view of revolution can be given a theological dimension. The God of the biblical revelation is a threat to a complacent establishment. The church as prophetic community must, with whatever unity and insight it can muster, be constant critic of its society. It must warn any government against the sin of presumption. All authority is from God and therefore answerable to him. All authority is for the service of men —and therefore judged when it becomes oppressive or neglectful. The church cannot grant uncritical consent to the exercise of state power. Order is a very great good which the church ought to affirm. But order without justice is an evil which the church must negate. Men may desire order so badly that they are willing to let its claim take precedence over all others. The church must retain the independence which lets it speak for the whole range of the needs and rights of men—of which the need for order is only one. The church is witness to the Christian message which stands over all the structures of human life as a continual demand for change—a call for "perpetual renovation."

But with this much said in behalf of revolution, the ambivalence of the force of revolution needs now to be considered. It is necessary to recognize that revolutions are not always right, and the governments they oppose are not always incurably oppressive. Change—even change brought about under high ideals and with a sense of urgency—is not always for the better. The worthy martyrs have not all been those who fell in the cause of revolution. No sympathy with revolutionary causes should encourage anyone to suppose that every time a coup takes place and a ruler is executed it is inevitably the Lord's doing and marvelous in our eyes. The argument which urges that revolutionary effort ought not to be categorically disallowed should not be overstated to say that revolutions ought categorically to be welcomed. One must be discriminating. "My revolution, right or wrong" is just as mistaken as "my government, right or wrong."

It was argued in the opening of Chapter Five that a person cannot be for civil disobedience in itself without reference to some large priorities or claims that might justify breaking the law. Disobedience can be used in a bad cause as readily as in a good cause. Similarly here where civil disobedience in a context of revolution is under consideration, it is necessary to ask large questions about purposes. Which revolution? How conducted?

The great requirement of any revolutionary cause is that—given the situation at the time—it analyze the issues acutely and represent, in the terms of the situation, the maximum possible justice. (History will probably settle for a revolution which at least represents significantly more justice than the power it sought to replace.) The righteous love of God is still the measure of all our actions—our bringing about of change as much as our maintenance of existing order. By their doctrinaire aims, their ruthless means, or their results unequal to the cost to gain them, some revolutions are condemned, just as tyrannical states are condemned.

There is a tendency for revolutions to narrow the range of human reality of which account is taken. They leave out the variousness and unexpectedness of life. They become their own justification. Revolutionary purpose can achieve humane goals only if it is realistic about the limitations set by the human condition. Admittedly, revolution is often moved by retaliatory hatred and is likely to be pushed to impulsive, irrational actions and uncontrolled excess. But such revolution is likely to undo its own intentions. A revolutionary force, in its own interests, ought to exercise self-restraint and observe some cautions:

1. Revolutionary effort tends to be utopian. It is so one-sided a cause that it can lose the sense of its own fallibility and corruptibility. Revolutionists can persuade themselves that once the oppressing institutions of society have been swept aside and their own forces have replaced the incumbents in power, the wrongs of human government will have been completely and forever put away.

The new regime cannot realistically expect to escape the shortsightedness and self-interest of the old. It may be unduly cynical to suggest that new orderings of the community are only rearrangements of its injustices. Some arrangements are definitely better than others. But the comment deserves a hearing. If a revolution simply intends to replace one oppressive ruling clique with another composed of victims of the earlier one, it can hardly command support on moral grounds. "That sort of thing won't be done any more because it will be 'us' in charge, and not 'them' " is most unpersuasive. Those who propose revolution must have made some analysis of the existing situation and its causes and have a general idea of what qualitatively different measures might prevent future tyranny. They must accept strong checks on power—including their own. Moreover, doctrines and institutions should contain the possibility of their own self-correction in the light of the realities of the actual community in operation.

2. The kind of effort required for a small part of society to bring about a change in government—tight control, secrecy, reduction of the area of debate—introduces qualities which are the contrary of those wanted in a free and open society. The skills developed in revolution may unfit their users for the task of sustained rule. The ideals of a disciplined band of revolutionists may not be those that should be carried over as the practice of a large, diversified populace. Thus, the experience of revolution can itself work against the emancipating aims with which the effort was begun. Unless the revolutionaries are aware of this possibility and take it into account, the new regime may end in tolerating less personal freedom than was allowed in the regime it deposed.

3. Revolutionaries are likely to exaggerate the discontinuity which is possible in human experience and institutions. By their theories and their experience they are likely to have identified the evils of the old regime and to have taken its better features for granted. Since they are not consciously aware of these benefits of the old system and of their own debt to them, they risk leaving them out of the explicit ordering of the new system—requiring some future generation to rediscover them and reinstate them, possibly by revolution.

Those engaged in revolution tend to overestimate the possibilities of human freedom. Changes can be brought about in the ordering of the community by deliberate decision, but the newness that can be introduced in history is partial at best. Such change as is sought ought to have modest goals which recognize the inevitable bonds that tie generation to generation and person to person in community.

4. As a precondition to attacking their government, revolutionaries have "signed off" from it. They deny its claim on themselves and their loyalty to it. Thoreau once gave the town clerk a note saying, "Know all men by these presents, that I,

Henry Thoreau, do not wish to be a member of any incorporated society which I have not joined." He adds, "If I had known how to name them, I should then have signed off in detail from all the societies which I never signed on to; but I did not know where to find a complete list." [8] But such disaffiliation from life's primary communities is only partially possible; our most important memberships in human groups are given in the very terms of life—though the extent of independent action possible for the individual has been increasing in recent generations. Any "declaration of independence" will witness by its very content and texture to the existing materials out of which it was made and whose influence cannot be denied.

5. The revolutionary has an inadequate sense of the vast unmanageability of history. Forces of revolution—set in motion by deliberate acts—introduce a great disruption into a society and loosen its traditional restraints and controls. The momentum of radical change is likely to carry on past the intentions of those who initiated the process. D. W. Brogan comments on the French Revolution: "It was more than distressing to see the Revolution devouring its own children. . . . To save the Republic it was necessary to imitate and surpass the crimes of the monarchy." [9] The first victim of revolution may well be the dreams and intentions of the original revolutionaries. It may be more difficult to stop a revolutionary process at a relatively desirable point than it is to get it started in the first place.

6. Revolutionary causes have a tendency to become obsessive. One can, paradoxically, become captive to revolution. He can become blinded to a large, varied human purpose by the very intensity which one single purpose requires. In such a situation, he forgets that he is a fallible creature answerable to the Lord of all history. The revolution itself has become his god; the cause has become his messiah. The old regime is the evil one; its system is sin. The triumph of the radical new

movement will be redemption. Thus the ambiguity of revolution is forgotten as one is swept up in it.

THE FINAL LOYALTY

The burden of these cautions is simply that any obedience a Christian gives to a revolutionary cause cannot be an unconditional obedience. He must be detached from even while he is involved in the revolutionary forces of his time. If, in the light of all he knows, revolution is the best of the choices open, revolution must be accepted and followed—loyally, determinedly, and even gladly. If open disobedience to the existing state is attendant on that revolutionary effort, disobedience must be used—wisely, effectively, and without personal animus. Just as a Christian in some circumstances would be a good and obedient citizen, he might also in different circumstances be a good revolutionary. But just as he would not surrender his ultimate loyalty to the state but keep himself free to question and to act on his conscience, so he would not surrender his ultimate loyalty to revolution. He would ask penetrating questions and stand ready to dissent (possibly discovering that revolutionists can be even more short with nonconformists than governments are). He would serve revolution (as in another situation he would serve the state) as long as by so doing he would serve God and man as they are known in Jesus Christ.

The final loyalty of a Christian is not to revolution *nor* to existing status. He is not an unqualified conservative; neither is he an unqualified revolutionary. A Christian's final loyalty is to the Kingdom of God. This Kingdom is sovereign participant in and shaper of the events of human history. It is a divine activity which establishes the order of men; but it is a divine activity which overturns the order of men. It is an act of God whose fullness is yet to come. Meanwhile, a Christian lives in constant loyalty to that Kingdom. His loyalty to institutions of society may seem inconstant indeed—at times actually traitorous. But a Christian is persuaded that in the Kingdom lies the fulfillment and the freedom-in-dependence of every human life and every human institution. With as much discernment and dedication as he has, he gives himself in obedience to that Kingdom.

Appendix one

: :

THOREAU AND
POLITICAL OBLIGATION

Throughout any discussion of resistance and disobedience to civil government, the name and work of Henry Thoreau are often pertinent. He was read and admired by both Gandhi and Martin Luther King, Jr. The very term "civil disobedience" has derived its currency from Thoreau's essay of that title—a title which, by the way, he did not himself give. Few of his political ideas were original; most of them were shared among his associates. Yet his statements on disobedience have remained living documents as those of his predecessors and contemporaries have not.

Thoreau conducted a passionate defense of the individual against organized society. Anyone who, in our more depersonalized mass society, sympathizes with such an intention cannot but recognize Thoreau's work—especially "Civil Disobedience," "Life without Principle," the speech "A Plea for Captain John Brown," and the relevant portions of *Walden*—as a landmark in the literature of the human spirit. Thoreau's social and political ideas are given a highly personal statement; the writer constantly injects himself into his expositions; doctrines are made believable through a man of great integrity. Thoreau understates. His own act of civil disobedience was not momentous, and he does not overdramatize his account of "My Prisons." Just as he stands outside his fellow townsmen and their affairs, so he seems to observe himself with a detached irony. Yet his intellectual power, his moral seriousness, his concentration on essentials, and his skill with language have made him an enduring teacher of conscience.

But it is not easy to determine exactly what Thoreau meant to teach about civil disobedience; the evidence is mixed.

He said, "I quietly declare war with the state, after my fashion." His fashion was indeed quiet. He failed to pay a portion (but only a portion) of his taxes and as a consequence spent one night in prison until the delinquent tax was paid for him. Thus he deliberately transgressed a law, and he acquiesced in the penalty for his noncompliance. He took pains to differentiate himself from "those who call themselves no-government men." Unlike them, he did not ask for no government but only for a better government. (He did say that a better government was what he asked *"at once"*—leaving open the possibility that later something more drastic might be asked. But he did not say explicitly that such was his ultimate request.) Moreover, Thoreau acknowledged that his government was, as governments go, not a contemptible specimen: "The Constitution, with all its faults, is very good; the law and the courts are very respectable; even this State and this American government are, in many respects, very admirable and rare things, to be thankful for."

He is even somewhat concerned lest his own character be defective because of his too great readiness to consent to the laws of the land. If a reader wants to look in Thoreau for expressions affirming government, loyalty, and obedience, he will be at least modestly rewarded for his pains.

Nonetheless, the manner of the man and the expressions of apparent support for government should not deceive. It was really war with the state that Thoreau declared. He mounted a critique that was tough-minded and thorough.

He wrote at a time when the governments he knew were, by the standards of subsequent totalitarianisms and bureaucracies, governments which governed least. Yet he found them unjust and oppressive:

Unjust laws exist: shall we be content to obey them or shall we endeavor to amend them, and obey them until we have succeeded, or shall we transgress them at once? . . . If the injustice . . . is of such a nature that it requires you to be the agent of injustice to another, then, I say, break the law. . . . What I have to do is to see, at any rate, that I do not lend myself to the wrong which I condemn.

As for adopting the ways which the State has provided for remedying the evil, I know not of such ways. They take too much time, and a man's life will be gone. I have other affairs to attend to.

These other affairs were primarily the business of being a man—a calling carried out apart from the state for the most part, but against the state when necessary. He asked that others answer to themselves and be men regardless of the expectations of society. "I think we should be men first, and subjects afterward." He considered the power of even a few such persons. "Action from principle,—the perception and the performance of right,—changes things and relations; it is essentially revolutionary."

But Thoreau's attitude went beyond counseling the disobedience of specific ordinances. He forswore any responsible relation to the state:

How does it become a man to behave toward this American government today? I answer, that he cannot without disgrace be associated with it. I cannot for an instant recognize that political organization as *my* government which is the *slave's* government also. . . .

I can afford to refuse allegiance to Massachusetts, and her right to my property and life. . . .

I simply wish to refuse allegiance to the State, to withdraw and stand aloof from it effectually. . . .

But Thoreau did more than register his withdrawal from a flawed political order. Behind his complaints of governmental injustices and blindness are more fundamental questions about the state itself. Thoreau announced in the first paragraph of

"Civil Disobedience" that a government which governed not at all would be even better than that government which governed least. The rest of the essay provides some evidence that the comment was more than a whimsical extension of his opening idea. He closes the same essay saying that he recognizes no governmental right over himself—at least no right which he has not first conceded to it. He wants the state to acknowledge the individual as "a higher and independent power" and to treat him as such. Thus there is a strong anarchical tendency throughout this essay and in Thoreau's political stance as a whole.

Insofar as these discrepant trends in Thoreau's thought are reconcilable, the matter might be formulated as follows: Thoreau's most extreme doctrines, rigorously pressed, constitute a gospel of anarchism. But they are not always understood as such by those who read and admire him. There is an ambiguity (probably quite deliberate) in his writing. Much is suggested that is not made fully explicit; ideas are dropped whose consequences are not explored; radical ideas and modest disclaimers are set side by side. Moreover, the style of the man keeps his anarchism from being identified; it is anarchism without street barricades. Thoreau admired and defended John Brown; but he was not himself a John Brown. He lived during two wars and much domestic tumult; yet he remained a quiet citizen of Concord—inspecting snowstorms, assisting at sunrises, and reading lectures on resistance to civil government to the Lyceum. His single act of open disobedience was carried out so as to inflict a minimum of inconvenience on himself and on the authorities. His tactic was not to assail the state, but quietly to withdraw. He was willing to come to those terms with the state that expediency might require—"I will still make what use and get what advantage of her I can." But he commented, "The government does not concern me much, and I shall bestow the fewest possible thoughts on it. It is not many moments that I live under a government." In general, Thoreau was not going to press his quarrel.

"I came into this world, not chiefly to make this a good place to live in, but to live in it, be it good or bad. A man has not every thing to do, but something; and because he cannot do *very thing,* it is not necessary that he should do *something* wrong." Even though his explicit critique of society went very deep, he expressed his own stance, not by reform but by dis-affiliation. He wrote, "Perhaps I am more than usually jealous with respect to my freedom. I feel that my connection with and obligation to society are still very slight and transient." (From "Life without Principle." The other passages quoted in this Appendix are all from "Civil Disobedience.")

Responsibility for existing social order or for its correction rested very lightly on Thoreau. Those who cite with gratitude his memorable words on disobedience are obliged, on Thoreau's own terms, to think for themselves. Thoreau seems to have considered disobedience largely as a tactic to dissociate him-self from complicity in social evil. He hoped for a time when organized structures of society would be done away. It would seem possible and not entirely unjust to accept much of the spirit and teaching of Thoreau without meaning in detail what he meant and without sharing his romantic hope. In the setting of New England Transcendentalism some things could be pro-posed that might not be comparably responsible if said now.

Appendix two

: :

CHURCH STATEMENTS ON
CIVIL DISOBEDIENCE

A widespread consensus on civil disobedience exists among major Christian groups. The vocabulary and emphasis with which the point is formulated differ from tradition to tradition. But on the central recognition of a moral right or duty to disobey the state when the situation requires, there is agreement among the ecclesiastical bodies which have declared themselves officially. A selection of ecumenical and denominational statements is given here.

THE VATICAN COUNCIL

The lengthy "Pastoral Constitution on the Church in the Modern World" issued by Vatican Council II touched on the subject. This document is addressed to humanity at large rather than to the Roman Church or the wider Christian community. This official pronouncement should be read in the context of the tradition of moral theology for which disobedience to an unjust law is a familiar and a carefully qualified teaching. The portions quoted here are from paragraph 74.

The political community exists for that common good in which the community finds its full justification and meaning, and from which it derives its pristine and proper right. . . .

Political authority, whether in the community as such or in institutions representing the state, must always be exercised within the limits of morality and on behalf of the dynamically conceived common good, according to a juridical order enjoying legal status. When such is the case citizens are conscience-bound to obey. This fact clearly reveals the responsibility, dignity, and importance of those who govern.

Where public authority oversteps its competence and oppresses the people, these people should nevertheless obey to the extent that the objective common good demands. Still it is lawful for them to defend their own rights and those of their fellow citizens against any abuse of this authority, provided that in so doing they observe the limits imposed by natural law and the gospel.

WORLD CONFERENCE ON CHURCH AND SOCIETY

The World Conference on Church and Society was held at Geneva in July, 1966, under the auspices of the World Council of Churches. There were participants from eighty nations and one hundred and sixty-four churches; a majority of them were laymen. The Official Report entitled "Christians in the Technical and Social Revolutions of Our Time" (published by the World Council of Churches, Geneva, 1967) sustains a high level of competence on a wide range of subjects. A portion dealing with the obedience and dissent of Christian citizens (Section II, par. 81–82) is cited here.

When Christians find themselves in a country in which the national life is based on a constitution which clearly guarantees human rights and dignity as understood by Christian faith and by universal consensus (UN Declaration of Human Rights), in which legislation is enacted in accordance with such a constitution, in which power is so exercised as to make this legislation effective, and in which adequate provision is made for orderly and periodic modification and improvement, they are called to act in political life within the provisions of such a system. They should support programmes of education in civic affairs, share their insights on public matters, help form a positive public opinion, and use fully their constitutional rights to support and implement the constitutional system, seeking also its progressive improvement.

But there is evidence that there are cases in which (1) constitutions do not offer adequate guarantees, (2) legislation often does not conform to the constitution, (3) the power structure renders a good constitution ineffective, or (4) no adequate means are available for effective change and amendment with reasonable speed. In many cases where legislation violates an acceptable constitution, and no speedy means of legal relief are available, the Christian may be called to civil disobedience (sit-down strikes, passive disobedience or deliberate violation of laws). In cases in which the constitution itself is inadequate, the Christian is called to work for its amendment in the interest of firmer guarantees of human rights. Where such changes are impossible, the Christian may come to the conclusion that he has no alternative but to violate the constitution in order to make possible a better one. We recognize a scale of values: human rights, constitution and legislation. We understand that laws may be defied in defence of the constitution, and that the constitution may be defied in the defence of human rights. The decision can only be made for each specific situation by those who are within it, with full awareness of the possible consequences. The Church should not withdraw fellowship from Christians who make such a decision.

THE NATIONAL COUNCIL OF CHURCHES

On June 7, 1968, the General Board of the National Council of Churches of Christ, U.S.A., adopted a policy statement on "Religious Obedience and Civil Disobedience." The issuance of this statement was noted in the press at the time, but the text itself seems not to have been widely reproduced. It is a well-unified, forceful statement and is given here in its entirety.

Policy Statement on

RELIGIOUS OBEDIENCE AND CIVIL DISOBEDIENCE

I. *Man Acts Politically*

Men are political creatures; they are seldom politically inert. Usually they act for their own political advantage or aggrandizement. Sometimes they act for the sake of principle or for the benefit of others, even to their own disadvantage. Often they act with mixed motives and effects. When they fail to act at all, they yield the ground to others, and thus share responsibility for the political outcome.

God calls men to act within and upon the structures of their time for the serving of their fellowmen. When they obey this calling, they are acting politically. Since most men act politically most of the time (if only by default), their religious obedience does not add a new kind of *action* so much as a new *direction*. Instead of acting politically for personal or partisan advantage, the man who seeks to obey God's calling tests all his actions by their effect on the whole commonwealth, particularly upon the disadvantaged, who are the special object of divine compassion.

He does not choose whether to act politically or not to act politically so much as whether to act obediently or not to act obediently to God's calling. Once a man's (political) course is set toward the serving of his fellowmen and away from serving his own advantage at the expense of his fellowmen, the mode or level of his (political) action will be determined by tactical and ethical considerations arising from his circumstance.

II. *The Range of Man's Action Based on Conscience*

The range of possible action is broad, and men seeking to obey God's will have chosen various modes of action at various times:

A. *Abstention.* Some Christians believe that they should not attempt, either individually or corporately or both, to influence the political structures of their time. (Their abstention, however, is not without effect—sometimes crucial effect—upon political events.)

B. *Action Within the Existing Structures of Civil Law and Government.* This is the most common mode of obedient action, particularly in modern democracies, for those citizens who share in determining the structures. It includes the kinds of action protected by the First Amendment of the U.S. Constitution—freedom of speech, freedom of press, freedom of assembly and petition (including orderly picketing)—which are thereby incorporated in the existing structures.

C. *Peaceable, Public Action in Opposition to a Particular Law or Policy.* When citizens support a democratic system of government in general, but oppose a particular law or policy they consider unjust, they sometimes resort to systematic civil disobedience of that law. (Even in a representative democracy there is often a lag between the frontiers of Christian conscience and some laws passed by the legislature, as in the case of laws upholding discrimination and segregation which after a century were acknowledged to be contrary to both Christian principles and the Constitution of the nation.)

D. *Action in Resistance to a Particular Law or Policy.* Political action which is *covert* (such as the Underground Railroad by which Quakers and others spirited escaped slaves to Canada) or *violent* is an option beyond the range of civil disobedience, though still directed against a limited target of felt injustice rather than against the existing structure as a whole.

E. *Action in Revolution Against an Entire System of Government.* Covert and violent action designed to overthrow the existing system of government altogether is *revolution* rather than *resistance,* and men seeking to obey the will of God have sometimes resorted to it for reasons such as those stated in the American *Declaration of Independence,* a historic manifesto of revolution.

We recognize that when justice cannot be secured either through action within the existing structures or through civil disobedience, as increasing number of Christians may feel called to seek justice through resistance or revolution. Therefore, a study should be made of alternatives of resistance and revolution in the light of Christian principles and experience.

III. *"We Must Obey God Rather than Man"*

In the tradition which shaped the American political system, it is generally agreed that the function of government is to secure justice, peace and freedom for its citizens, and to maintain order, not as an end in itself, but as a condition necessary for the existence of justice, peace and freedom. Christians find this tradition generally compatible with their understanding of the divinely-ordained function of the state.

When, however, a particular government fails to provide justice, peace or freedom, it is not maintaining true order, and Christians should remain faithful to their understanding of what order ought to be, even at the cost of disobeying that government. In such circumstances, it is the government which has become insubordinate to God's order, and not those who disobey that government. Rather, they show their genuine respect for rightful "governing authority" by criticizing, resisting or opposing the current misusers of that authority.

Although Christians recognize the importance of order for human society, in every period of history there has been a Christian witness against giving absolute or unquestioning obedience to any civil authority. The first allegiance of Christians is to God, and when earthly rulers command what is contrary to the will of God, Christians reply as did Peter and John, "We must obey God rather than men." (Acts 5:29). Whatever the penalty for disobedience to human law, it has not deterred some Christian martyrs in every age from pointing by their death beyond man's order to God's order.

IV. Conscience: One and Many

At no time, however, have Christians been unanimous in agreeing how or when they should "obey God rather than men." The essential problem is to determine when the state represents God's instrument of order and when it represents man's tyranny. The decision is a fateful one, and Christians have taken it only with reluctance.

Individual conscience, though more sensitive than the aggregate of men, is often eccentric, obsessive or obtuse, and needs the correction that can come from sympathetic encounter with the conscience of others. Both individual and group can benefit by supportive confrontation within the religious community: the individual may become aware of countervailing facts and factors, and the community may find its equanimity disturbed by the anguish of the individual.

Since the warning of the need for change comes to and through individual conscience, the community should safeguard its expression, however strident or abrasive it may seem. A more acute problem is posed for the community when the protesting conscience progresses from dialogue to demonstration, from conversation to civil disobedience. Then the community is inclined to chide the dissenter with having gone too far, with having somehow exceeded the bounds of conduct permissible to Christians. Yet the briefest reflection on history will remind us that this judgment is not accurate. Some of the most venerated Christian saints and sages have spent part of their lives in prison or have been banished or executed for defying the civil authorities of their time, and this was not a reproach to them but a sign of their obedience to God.

V. *Witness: Words and Deeds*

Civil law in the United States distinguishes between speech and action. Acts which violate the law can be punished, but speech cannot unless it poses a "clear and present danger" to public safety. This distinction in law and jurisprudence has proved to be a valuable safeguard of the rights to free communication of ideas. Christian theology, however, does not recognize such a dichotomy between the witness of word and deed, for the former without the latter is "hypocrisy." The Christian who is impelled to speak against an unjust law is not necessarily excused from action because of civil interdiction. He is responsible before God for his deeds as well as his words, and cannot yield that responsibility to anyone, even to the magistrate.

VI. *Civil Disobedience: Its Role and Operation*

Civil disobedience is used in this statement to mean deliberate, peaceable violation of a law deemed to be unjust, in obedience to conscience or a higher law, and with recognition of the state's legal authority to punish the violator.

A. Civil disobedience is *deliberate*. It is consciously willed and intended, based on deep conviction, and entered into with full awareness of the consequences, after the failure of less disruptive alternatives. Violation of law through ignorance or inadvertence is not civil disobedience.

B. Civil disobedience is *public*. There is no effort to conceal it from the authorities; on the contrary, they are often given advance notice of intended acts of civil disobedience. Even when such advance notice is not given, one result of civil disobedience frequently is to focus public awareness on injustice by overt acts of disobedience.

C. Civil disobedience is *peaceable*. It seeks to minimize the harm done to others through willingness to suffer hurt rather than to inflict it. A criminal action, for instance, is one by which the perpetrator harms the commonwealth for his own advantage, whereas in civil disobedience the perpetrator seeks to benefit the commonwealth at his own risk and disadvantage.

D. Civil disobedience is *violation of a law deemed to be unjust* in obedience to conscience or a higher law. It is usually entered into by those who feel they have no choice but to disobey—as Luther put it, "Here I stand, God help me. *I can do no other.*" The authority appealed to beyond civil statutes may be God's commandments, the moral law, natural law, the good of mankind or some other norm of conscience for which one is willing, even compelled, to risk offending civil authorities and public opinion.

E. Civil disobedience entails *recognition of the state's legal authority to punish those who violate the law*. In a society in which the man who seeks to obey God can honor and subordinate himself to the civil order as a whole, and is compelled by conscience to disobey only one law or group of laws, he will recognize the state's power to punish violators of the law, including himself. If the government or the civil order as a whole is so corrupt or demonic that to criticize any aspect of it is to court death as an enemy of the regime (as was the case in Hitler's Germany), then the Christian may reluctantly conclude that he cannot willingly recognize or submit to the state's power to punish at all, in which case he is engaged, not in civil disobedience, but in civil resistance or revolution with which this statement does not attempt to deal.

The foregoing is a description of the form of civil disobedience exemplified by Henry David Thoreau, Leo Tolstoy, Mohandas Gandhi, and Martin Luther King, Jr. So understood, it is a limited and moderate mode of political action, and we call upon Christians and other men of good will to recognize it as a valid instrument for those who seek justice, consonant with both Christian tradition and the American political and legal heritage.

VII. *Response of the Church to Civil Disobedience*

The Christian Church owes to its members who undertake civil disobedience the following measures of support:

A. Pastoral and material care of the individual and of his family;

B. Exploration and testing of the individual's views within the Christian community;

C. Interpretation of the moral legitimacy of the individual's position, even if the majority of the Church does not agree with him;

D. Protection of his legal rights, including the right to counsel;

E. Pursuit of judicial review or amendment of unjust statutes;

F. Enactment of laws more nearly conformable to moral principles.

LUTHERAN CHURCH IN AMERICA

In 1964 the Second Biennial Convention of the Lutheran Church in America adopted a rather full statement on "Race Relations," one portion of which dealt with civil disobedience. That portion, however, was carefully written and can stand by itself.

Christians are committed to the rule of law as an expression of the moral law of God. Nevertheless, it must be recognized that laws have been and may in the future be enacted, or social customs may exist, which are believed to be in basic conflict with the constitutional law of the land or the moral law of God. In such circumstances, the church, its congregations, synods, agencies and institutions, including their representatives, as well as individual members, are recognized as free by all lawful means including peaceful public demonstrations, to urge repeal or invalidation of such laws or to effect change of such customs.

If and when the means of legal recourse have been exhausted or are demonstrably inadequate, Christians may then choose to serve the cause of racial justice by disobeying a law that clearly involves the violation of their obligations as Christians, so long as they are

a. willing to accept the penalty for their action;

b. willing to limit and direct their protest as precisely as possible against a specific grievance or injustice;

c. willing to carry out their protest in a nonviolent, responsible manner, after earnestly seeking the counsel of fellow Christians and the will of God in prayer.

In all of this, we are guided and supported by the normative teaching of the church in Article XVI of the Augsburg Confession: "Christians are obliged to be subject to civil authority and obey its commands and laws in all that can be done without sin. But when commands of the civil authority cannot be obeyed without sin, 'we must obey God rather than men' " (Acts 5:29).

PRESBYTERIAN CHURCH IN THE UNITED STATES

At its 106th General Assembly in 1966, the Southern Presbyterian Church adopted a carefully qualified statement on civil disobedience. It contains an unusually full defense of a rule of law and of the citizen's obligation to obey. Yet it recognizes that grievous abuses can corrupt governmental processes by depriving citizens of their rights and of their normal means of appeal. As a final resort, citizens in such a situation may turn to civil disobedience. The statement concludes:

This measure can be justified only under most pressing necessity. But when such a situation prevails the church may properly support those using this means to obtain for themselves those unalienable rights with which all men are endowed by their Creator.

The Church can take the above position upon the biblical ground which demands that every man's primary allegiance must be to God Almighty. Her proclamation through the ages has been, and should continue to be, that God alone is Lord, not only over every individual conscience, but also over every human institution.

To sum up: The Presbyterian Church, U.S., desires at this time to reaffirm the obligation of all her obedient sons and daughters: (1) To live responsibly under the law of the land; (2) To use personal influence and ballot to enhance the rule of law so that injustice may be replaced with justice, and the full provisions of the law for justice, protection, and liberty may be enjoyed by every citizen of every community; (3) To regard civil disobedience as a measure of last resort to be employed only in circumstances of otherwise irremediable need, and in the exercise of which the whole concept of law is not denied, but affirmed; and (4) To continue to support and regard with compassion those who practice civil disobedience when no legal recourse has been left open to them and who act in Christian conscience and allegiance to Almighty God.

THE PROTESTANT EPISCOPAL CHURCH

At the General Convention of the Episcopal Church in 1964 a brief but careful statement on civil disobedience originated in the House of Bishops where it was passed by a large majority. It was submitted in the House of Deputies where (in a "vote by orders") it was approved by the clergy by a substantial majority but lost decisively in the lay vote. Hence the resolution lost in the House and the Convention. The division on an important ethical issue shown by this vote was exceedingly painful at the time. The statement on civil disobedience was later issued by the House of Bishops as a position paper for the advice of the clergy. It is given here in its entirety:

> Christian teaching holds that civil authority is given by God to provide order in human society, and that just human law is a reflection of immutable divine law which man did not devise. Under all normal circumstances, therefore, Christians obey the civil law, seeing in it the will of God. Yet it must be recognized that laws exist which deny these eternal and immutable laws. In such circumstances, the Church and its members, faithful to Scripture, reserve the right to obey God rather than man.
>
> Thus the Church recognizes the rights of any persons to urge the repeal of unjust laws by all lawful means, including participation in *peaceful* demonstrations. If and when the means of legal recourse have been exhausted, or are demonstrably inadequate, the Church recognizes the right of all persons, for reasons of informed conscience, to disobey such laws, so long as such persons
>
> a) accept the legal penalty for their action,
> b) carry out their protest in a non-violent manner, and
> c) exercise severe restraint in using this privilege of conscience, because of the danger of lawlessness attendant thereon.
>
> Before Christians participate in such actions, they should seek the will of God in prayer and the counsel of their fellow Christians.

THE UNITED METHODIST CHURCH

At its General Conference on May 3, 1968, the United Methodist Church adopted a forceful statement on "the Rule of Law and the Right of Dissent." The statement opens with a recognition of the circumstances which give urgency to these topics. Part One of the statement is on the necessity of law but also the recognition that legal structures must be watched to see that they continue to serve rather than obstruct justice. Part Two is on the right and value of responsible dissent. Part Three is specifically on civil disobedience, and Part Four deals with the counseling of persons on problems of conscience.

Three, We affirm the right of non-violent civil disobedience in extreme cases as a viable option in a democracy and as a sometime requirement for Christians who are to have no other God than the God of Jesus Christ. By civil disobedience we mean the deliberate and non-violent disobeying of a law believed to be unjust or unconstitutional, and the willingness to accept penalties for that violation.

Where a civil disobedient has a fundamental respect for legal institutions of society and is prepared to accept penalties for disobedience, there is little threat to the basic concept of the rule of law.

We believe that such disobedience under conscientious control does not justify, nor would it encourage, widespread casual and indiscriminate violation of law. Some may misinterpret the civil disobedient's motivation and action, and respond accordingly; but this is one of the risks that must be taken in a society that gives some autonomy to an informed and sensitive conscience. We believe that not only the individual who protests, but freedom of religion and the best interests of the society itself, will be served by this freedom for conscientious action.

THE UNITED PRESBYTERIAN CHURCH IN THE U.S.A.

At its 178th General Assembly in 1966 the United Presbyterian Church in the U.S.A. adopted a number of brief statements related to student activity in social protest. Some of these touch on the general issue of civil disobedience:

The 178th General Assembly

1. Affirms the right of students to engage in responsible political discussion and activity as an aspect of their participation in a democratic society and as a dimension of their education;

2. Urges every citizen conscientiously to obey the law and to support policies of government; but when impelled by conscience, to advocate alternatives to the law, to criticize and to dissent from laws and policies, to remonstrate, to seek modification and change, and only as a last resort to practice conscientious disobedience, realizing the serious responsibility placed upon those who disobey, and accepting the legal consequences of such conscientious disobedience;

3. Cautions all public officials, editors, news commentators, and others against lumping together and indiscriminately labeling critics of governmental policies as un-American, or portraying protesters as immoral or mentally unbalanced without presenting responsible evidence; . . .

6. Affirms the right of all persons engaged in criticism or protest to protection from brutality, intimidation, or reprisal from any source; . . .

Appendix three
: :
DISOBEDIENCE AND
THE LEGAL PENALTY

Over the generations the tradition has been sustained that when one is civilly disobedient, he accepts the legal penalty for his act. Similarly it has been argued that the government is required, by its very nature and function, to exact the assigned punishment. This point is stated in these traditional terms in Chapter Six (see pp. 101–122) of the present book among the conditions of responsible disobedience. But there seem now to be reasons for some qualifications and second thoughts which will be sketched here outside the main argument of the book.

The classic assumption that punishment is properly consequent upon deliberate disobedience is very old. In Sophocles' drama, Antigone admits that she had known of the king's decree; it had been well publicized. She did not disobey through ignorance. She makes no attempt to deny her act. Creon argues that he would be less than a man and a king if he could be thus disobeyed with impunity. Antigone inquires, "Do you want more than my arrest and death?" Creon says that he does not. Antigone then asks, "Why are you waiting?"

The point is given a fuller articulation in Plato's *Crito*. In this dialogue, Socrates is under sentence and awaiting execution. He is visited in prison by his wealthy friend Criton, who urges Socrates to take the opportunity and flee Athens; the help of Criton and others of Socrates' followers is pledged. Escape would be easy. But Socrates does not use the opportunity.

177

He argues that were he to consider escaping, the Laws of the city would remonstrate with him. He would hear them reminding him of his bonds with and debt to the city. The Laws would contend that they have given him so much that he has no equal rights against them. If private persons could overturn duly imposed sentences, they would have attacked the state which begot them. The Laws ask whether Socrates really intends to destroy the commonwealth. Moreover, he has had opportunity to leave the city all his life, but he has not done so; by remaining, he has contracted an obligation to the institutions of Athens. The Laws say to Socrates:

> If any one of you (citizens) remains (in the city), when he sees in what manner we decide lawsuits and manage other public business, we say that he has now agreed in fact to do whatever we command; and we say that the disobedient man does wrong in three ways when he disobeys us: firstly, because we are his parents, secondly, because we are his nurturers, and thirdly, because he agreed to obey us and neither obeys us nor convinces us if we do anything not right. (Rouse trans.)

Socrates voluntarily remained in Athens and accepted the sentence of death. The argument of the *Crito* is very important. Many (probably most) of those who have disobeyed laws in conscience and received the penalty have had no choice about the penalty. Their acceptance with dignity of the punishment appointed for their act has not been without moral significance. But it is of exceptional value to have this account of the philosophical reasons which held Socrates in Athens when he might have fled. He argues that acceptance of his sentence is owed to the state; it is his affirmation of the order of the community and his acknowledgment of its rightful claim on him even while he rejects the justice of his own condemnation.

Civil disobedients over the centuries, insofar as they have had opportunity to reflect, would probably have given an account of themselves along lines forged by Socrates. Their disobedience was a No to a specific unjust measure; their acceptance of the punishment was a Yes to the community.

Thoreau's refusal to pay his tax and his consequent night in prison is sometimes cited as standing in this tradition. But the differences between Socrates' attitude and Thoreau's are certainly more fundamental than are any similarities in conduct. Thoreau had no piety toward Concord comparable to Socrates' toward Athens. No Laws of Massachusetts spoke to Thoreau stating a claim which he felt bound to acknowledge. Rather:

> I could not help being struck with the foolishness of that institution which treated me as if I were mere flesh and blood and bones, to be locked up. . . . I saw that the State was half-witted, that it was timid as a lone woman with her silver spoons, and that it did not know its friends from its foes, and I lost all my remaining respect for it, and pitied it. ("Civil Disobedience")

Moreover, Thoreau offers no account of a purpose in his imprisonment. In one tantalizing passage he does say, "Under a government which imprisons any unjustly, the true place for a just man is also a prison." But he does not fill out any connected ideas clarifying the link between justness and imprisonment. After his own night in prison he resumed his appointment as guide to a huckleberry party. Socrates' appointment was with hemlock.

Mohandas Gandhi, on the other hand, was more than loyal to the Socratic tradition. His civil disobedience was not a matter of individual conscience; it became under his leadership a mass social weapon. At a trial in March, 1922, he was permitted to make a statement prior to sentencing. With great dignity he consented to all the accusations in the case against him. He admitted that some demonstrations instigated by him and his movement had gone to excess and violated his intentions. He accepted responsibility for these terrible disorders and asked the court not only for a penalty, but for the highest penalty. He even took occasion to instruct the judge that it was his duty to administer such a sentence:

I wanted to avoid violence, I want to avoid violence. Non-violence is the first article of my faith. It is also the last article of my creed. But I had to make my choice. I had either to submit to a system which I considered had done irreparable harm to my country, or incur the risk of the mad fury of my people bursting forth when they understood the truth from my lips. I know that my people have sometimes gone mad. I am deeply sorry for it and I am therefore here to submit not to a light penalty but to the highest penalty. I do not ask for mercy. I do not plead any extenuating act. I am here, therefore, to invite and cheerfully submit to the highest penalty that can be inflicted upon me for what in law is a deliberate crime and what appears to me to be the highest duty of a citizen. The only course open to you, the Judge, is, . . . either to resign your post, or inflict on me the severest penalty, if you believe that the system and law you are assisting to administer are good for the people. (Text available many places; here from Peter Mayer, ed., *The Pacifist Conscience,* pp. 210f.)

This classic tradition that the civil disobedient must be prepared to pay the penalty informed the work of Martin Luther King, Jr. He wrote from Birmingham jail:

In no sense do I advocate evading or defying the law, as would the rabid segregationist. That would lead to anarchy. One who breaks an unjust law must do so openly, lovingly, and with a willingness to accept the penalty. I submit that an individual who breaks a law that conscience tells him is unjust, and who willingly accepts the penalty of imprisonment in order to arouse the conscience of the community over its injustice, is in reality expressing the highest respect for law.

Much of this tradition would seem to remain intact. Different as were the situations of Socrates and of Gandhi and different as were the ideological commitments of Socrates, Gandhi, and King, yet the simple connection of ethical ideas continues to make sense. The acceptance of legal punishment expresses a loyalty to the order of the community which is necessary to the moral case of the disobedient. (That loyalty has been obscured by the public violation of a law; the acceptance of the proper penalty clarifies it.) By such conduct the honor of the law has not suffered, and prison has been dignified.

Yet some further discussion seems called for. Questions might justifiably be raised about the presumed necessity that the disobedient accept punishment. There is certainly a symbolic value in the imprisonment of a Ghandhi or a King. It witnesses (dove fashion) to their moral seriousness, to the willingness of aggrieved persons to accept rather than inflict suffering, and to their acknowledgment of the order of the community. But also it can bring about (serpent fashion) some awkwardness and embarrassment for the authorities. The imprisonment of nonviolent leaders whose moral stature is widely respected can land the authorities in a sea of troubles. Moral condemnation and outside pressure to accommodate the protest can fall on those who make such an arrest. In other words, there are considerations of tactics and of public witness which are involved in accepting punishment for disobedience.

But these factors are not as forceful in the case of followers as they are in the case of leaders. Inasmuch as civil disobedience has frequently, since Gandhi, become a weapon of mass social protest more than a decision of individual conscience, it may be important to ask to what extent the thinking about the meaning of punishment articulated by a Socrates, a Gandhi, or a King should apply to the many largely anonymous persons who associate themselves in actions of protest. Obviously in many cases much of the same thinking would apply unchanged. The meaning of the leaders has been caught by the followers; the intentions of an aggrieved group have been articulated by the leaders. The mass following lacks the symbolic personal significance of the leader, but in solidarity with him, it can add the eloquence of numbers. "Fill the jails" can be a profound expression of corporate dedication, and it will be heard as a staggering threat by the authorities. If the authorities attempt to isolate a few leaders and make the punishment fall largely on them, it may be that the less conspicuous persons associated with the protest will want to say in effect, "We too shared in the disobedience. Anything they did, we did. We accepted the same legal jeopardy with them. Any punishment administered to them must be administered to us as well. You must reckon with all of us." Authorities will sometimes say that it is their duty to arrest and prosecute, but that tactically they will decide to let some persons go. Disobedients may, in return, tactically decide that they must inform the authorities that it is their duty to arrest and prosecute all.

But, apart from numbers, those participants in civil disobedience who are not M. K. Gandhis or Martin Luther Kings can have real weakness. They may be vulnerable to the power of government arrayed for their arrest and conviction. They may lack the financial and legal resources to appeal excessive bail or sentencing or to appeal a trial swayed by local passion against nonconformists. They may lack the access to mass media of communication which would give their story a public hearing. The forces of the state will have control of the situation and can use their power to direct attention away from the central issue being raised by the disobedience (often an issue on which the state shows up badly) and on to diversionary issues.

When such conditions prevail, a disobedient may well feel that they qualify, in some measure, the obligation to suffer the penalty for his act. It may seem that the same corruption of the soul of the community which has led to the writing of an unjust law has also flawed its ability to treat fairly those who question such a law. If the organized processes of the community are all of a piece, noncompliance with a law may suggest noncompliance with the assignment of a penalty. A disobedient might be willing to accept the just penalty for his action, but what is he to do when he is persuaded that that is unobtainable?

From the point of view of the disobedient himself the problem of punishment might be summarized by saying: A person ought to break a law, when he must, willing and prepared to accept the penalty the community attaches to such an act. For tactical reasons he might seek the due penalty, but he need not do so. He ought to prepare a legal defense and use counsel to keep the issues on the focus he has chosen (to the extent that that is in his control) and to protect his legal rights. He may find his distrust of the official ways of the community heightened by his experience of the assigning and administering of punishment. The same argument which says that unjust laws need not be obeyed says that unjust punishment need not go unprotested. The same kinds of qualifications which hedge the disobedience of law so that it is a responsible and effective act would urge that appeal of misuse of the punitive power of the state be made within the legal structures themselves to the extent possible. But protest must be made.

Just as it has been argued classically that the disobedient must accept punishment, it has been argued that the state must punish. The point was recently put by Justice Fortas in this way:

Let me first be clear about a fundamental proposition. The motive of civil disobedience, whatever its type, does not confer immunity for law violation. Especially if the civil disobedience involves violence or a breach of public order prohibited by statute or ordinance, it is the state's to arrest the dissident. If he is properly arrested, charged, and convicted, he should be punished by fine or imprisonment, or both, in accordance with the provisions of law, unless the law is invalid in general or as applied.

He may be motivated by the highest moral principles. He may be passionately inspired. He may, indeed, be right in the eyes of history or morality or philosophy. These are not controlling. It is the state's duty to arrest and punish those who violate the laws designed to protect private safety and public order. (*Concerning Dissent and Civil Disobedience*, p. 32. Quoted with permission.)

But just as there seem to be possible qualifications tending to say that not every disobedient must always accept any punishment which happens to be assigned, there are qualifications which would say that the state is under no categorical necessity of exacting punishment. The state's right to punish disobedience of its laws is not in question. But it need not invariably exercise that right.

This case was put very ably in an article, "On Not Prosecuting Civil Disobedience," by Ronald Dworkin, in *The New York Review of Books,* June 6, 1968 (quoted with permission). The thesis of the article is contained in the following paragraph:

> The argument that, because the government believes a man has committed a crime, it must prosecute him is much weaker than it seems. Society "cannot endure" if it tolerates all disobedience; it does not follow, however, nor is there evidence, that it will collapse if it tolerates some. In the United States prosecutors have discretion whether to enforce criminal laws in particular cases. A prosecutor may properly decide not to press charges if the lawbreaker is young, or inexperienced, or the sole support of a family, or is repentant, or turns state's evidence, or if the law is unpopular or unworkable or generally disobeyed, or if the courts are clogged with more important cases, or for dozens of other reasons. This discretion is not license—we expect prosecutors to have good reasons for exercising it—but there are, at least *prima facie,* some good reasons for not prosecuting those who disobey the draft laws out of conscience. One is the obvious reason that they act out of better motives than those who break the law out of greed or a desire to subvert government. Another is the practical reason that our society suffers a loss if it punishes a group that includes—as the group of draft dissenters does—some of its most thoughtful and loyal citizens. Jailing such men solidifies their alienation from society, and alienates many like them who are deterred by the threat.

This argument seems entirely convincing. It is a significant modification of a point which had long gone without adequate questioning. It calls for no new laws or new procedures, but only for the humane use of an existing range of discretion in the exercise of rightful powers.

The sum of these matters is that a civil disobedient has done an act which the state has a right to punish and for which he stands willing to accept the legal penalty. But the disobedient is under no formal compulsion to undergo punishment, and the state is under no compulsion to exercise its acknowledged right. A disobedient can, when required, affirm the order of the community in other ways than submitting to a penalty which he can only regard as compounding the crimes of the state. The state can, when desirable, find more sensitive measures than imprisonment for those whose principal intention in violating a law is to encourage the state in a process of self-correction according to its own professed ideals.

Author's Notes

: :

1. What the Issue Is and Is Not

1. Martin Luther King, Jr., *Why We Can't Wait* (New York: Signet Books, 1964), pp. 69ff.

2. Charles Frankel, *The Love of Anxiety* (New York: Harper & Row, 1965), p. 172. Chapter XII of this book, from which this formulation is taken, was first published in *The New York Times Magazine* as "Is It Ever Right to Break the Law?"

3. St. Gregory on *The Pastoral Charge*, III, iv. (Bramley, trans. and ed.).

4. George F. Kennan, "Rebels without a Program," in *The New York Times Magazine*, January 21, 1968, p. 71. Quoted with permission. This article by Mr. Kennan evoked an extensive correspondence, principally from students. The original article, some of the letters to the author, and a rejoinder by Kennan have been issued in book form: George F. Kennan, *Democracy and the Student Left* (Boston: Atlantic-Little, Brown, 1968).

5. King, *op. cit.*, p. 84.

6. It should be observed, if only in a footnote, that only within quite recent decades would it have occurred to anyone to make this positive judgment on the role of courts. For the greater part of American history, the business of government in all its branches was carried on with little regard for social needs. Recognition of rights and dignities, and participation in power, were not extended or guaranteed; they had to be claimed, fought for, and taken by main force. Certainly after the collapse of Reconstruction in 1877, the Negro had to wait still another seventy-five years for recognition in legislation or court opinion. If in the shabby record of that time,

the courts were as a whole no less captive of the community of white owners and managers than was the rest of government, the Supreme Court at least can boast a striking succession of humane and prophetic opinions offered by courageous justices often in lonely dissent. The story of those disgraceful years is documented, at least with reference to one issue, in Ch. 6, "The Supreme Court and the Negro," of Rayford W. Logan's *The Betrayal of the Negro* (New York: Collier Books, 1965; originally published in 1954 as *The Negro in American Life and Thought: The Nadir, 1877–1901*). If significant advances have been made in recent years—often with courts ahead of legislatures and executives—the gains only begin to redress generations of ill-use. Since these gains are alterations in long-established patterns of unequal treatment, they are neither understood nor accepted by many in the community. These moves to admit more of society into the American dream seem to many people to be innovations which are up for review. There is real risk that such gains will be rescinded or will, like good acts before them (including even constitutional amendments), be allowed to lapse through inadequate implementation or official local noncompliance which will be allowed to go unrebuked at the federal level.

7. The report is contained in *Hearings Before the United States Commission on Civil Rights* (Hearings Held in Jackson, Mississippi, February 16–21, 1965), Vol. I, "Voting," pp. 22ff. The quoted words are on pages 24 and 18 of the volume. The results of these hearings were compiled in a book called *Law Enforcement: A Report on Equal Protection in the South*. This book, plus a similar, smaller volume, *Voting in Mississippi* (both issued by the U.S. Civil Rights Commission in 1965), are horrifying documents in their own right, and together they provide abundant material for reflection by anyone inclined to say that American governmental institutions can be counted on to correct themselves and that resort to civil disobedience is always impetuous.

8. John C. Bennett, "The Columbia Revolution: II," in *Christianity and Crisis*, June 24, 1968, pp. 138f. Quoted with permission.

9. Anthony Lewis, "Official Lawlessness in the South," in Henry Steele Commager (ed.), *The Struggle for Racial Equality* (New York: Harper Torchbooks, 1967), pp. 173f. Quoted with permission.

10. Henry Steele Commager, *Freedom and Order* (New York: Meridian Books, 1966), p. 287. Quoted with permission.

2. THE NEW TESTAMENT ON THE STATE

1. John C. Bennett, "The Place of Civil Disobedience," in *Christianity and Crisis,* December 25, 1967, p. 299. Dr. Bennett refers specifically to the words of Romans 13.

2. *Ibid.*

3. G. W. H. Lampe, "Secularization in the New Testament and the Early Church," in *Theology,* Vol. LXXI, No. 574 (April, 1968), p. 169. Quoted with permission.

4. Ethelbert Stauffer, *New Testament Theology,* trans. J. Marsh (New York: Macmillan, 1955), p. 197. Quoted with permission. Stauffer gives an interesting list of prayers for the state which can be found in the literature of the early church.

5. Cullmann's viewpoint is most accessible in his *The State in the New Testament* (New York: Scribners, 1956), pp. 56ff. and especially pp. 95ff. The same thesis is carefully worked out in Clinton D. Morrison, *The Powers That Be,* "Studies in Biblical Theology" No. 29 (London: SCM, 1960).

6. A guide to the literature of the discussion can be found in a long footnote by Dr. Reumann in John Reumann and William Lazareth, *Righteousness and Society* (Philadelphia: Fortress Press, 1967), p. 101. Reumann rejects Cullmann's position, as does C. K. Barrett in his careful commentary on Romans.

If Cullmann's interpretation of the "powers" is mistaken here, perhaps Romans 13 does not speak of the state as a manifestation of the principalities and powers, but as a protection against them. In that case, a parallel might be drawn with II Thessalonians 2 in which the role of restrainer against lawlessness may be the state's role. If this is a role in which St. Paul casts the Roman empire (and there is conjecture in this interpretation), it would add this early passage as another strong Pauline Yes to the state.

7. See on the point: G. B. Caird, *Principalities and Powers* (Oxford: Clarendon Press, 1956) for a descriptive study of Pauline thought; H. Berkhof, *Christ and the Powers,* trans. J. H. Yoder (Scottdale, Pa.: Herald Press, 1962) for a fine biblically informed

theological study; Albert van den Heuvel, *These Rebellious Powers* (London: SCM, 1966) for a powerful statement of the implications of the biblical theme.

8. Herbert Hensley Henson, *Christian Morality* (Oxford: Clarendon Press, 1936), p. 247.

9. M. R. Newbolt, *The Book of Unveiling* (London: S.P.C.K., 1952), p. 136.

10. The point is developed in R. H. Preston and A. T. Hanson, *The Revelation of St. John the Divine,* in the Torch Series (London: SCM, 1957), pp. 96ff.

11. Similarly an unreconciled Yes and No stand side by side in the Old Testament account of the establishment of the Hebrew monarchy. The general account of Saul's selection, anointing, and ultimate recognition as king regards the development as providential (I Samuel 9–11). But another account (I Samuel 7:3–8:22 and 10:17–27) regards the development as a rejection of God, which Samuel warns against.

12. The biblical survey portion of this work had been formulated using the categories of Yes and No when Professor Reumann mentioned in a conversation his own development of the topic along similar lines—but using a third category "somewhere between the 'Yes' and the 'No.'" The presence here of this very valuable third category—but not the development of the discussion under any of these categories—is indebted to Dr. Reumann's insight. His own exposition of these themes can now be found in *Righteousness and Society,* pp. 100–104.

13. C. H. Dodd, *The Epistle of Paul to the Romans,* in the Moffatt series (New York: Harper & Row, n.d.), p. 203.

14. Günther Bornkamm, *Jesus of Nazareth,* trans. McLuskey and Robinson (New York: Harper & Row, 1960), p. 120.

15. Sherman E. Johnson, *Jesus in His Homeland* (New York: Scribners, 1957), p. 103. Quoted with permission.

16. *Ibid.,* pp. 109f.

17. This interpretation of the saying on the tribute money is found in David Cairns, *The Image of God in Man* (New York: Philosophical Library, 1953), p. 30 and Bornkamm, *op. cit.,* p. 123. See also Dorothy L. Sayers, *The Man Born to Be King* (London: Gollancz, 1949), p. 225. In an address "A Call for Ecumenical

Polemics," published in *Religious Education*, March–April, 1967, Rabbi Eugene B. Borowitz cites (pp. 108f.) the Talmud as saying "When a king of flesh and blood stamps his likeness upon coins, they are identical, but when the Holy One Blessed Be He puts his image on all men, each one comes out unique."

18. One account describes the reactions of the churches to the rise of Nazism in terms of this biblically based duality: "Painful conflicts break out more and more not only between the orders of these [governmental] authorities and the commandments of God, but also (as it first appears) between the divine commandments themselves, i.e. between God's commandment to obey the authorities (Rom. xiii) and the commandment 'to obey God rather than men' (Acts v, 29)." Edmund Schlink, "The Witness of the German Church Struggle," in *Man's Disorder and God's Design* (New York: Harper & Row, n.d.), Part I, p. 97.

3. THE TRADITION OF CHRISTIAN DISSENT (1)

1. Elizabeth Wyckoff trans., in *The Complete Greek Tragedies* (Chicago: University of Chicago Press, 1959), Vol. II, p. 174. Quoted with permission.

2. Plato "Apology," 29f. W.H.D. Rouse trans., in *Great Dialogue of Plato* (New York: New American Library, 1956; Mentor Book). Quoted with permission.

3. Daniel 3:17f. There is striking witness to the persistence of the biblical tradition in Martin Luther King's "Letter from Birmingham Jail" where he cites a list of civil disobedients in history and begins: "Of course, there is nothing new about this kind of civil disobedience. It was evidenced sublimely in the refusal of Shadrach, Meshach and Abednego to obey the laws of Nebuchadnezzar."

4. The place of martyrdom in Judaism is ably summarized in W. H. C. Frend, *Martyrdom and Persecution in the Early Church* (New York: Doubleday, 1967), pp. 22–57. The biblical texts and theological interpretations from Jewish tradition are gathered in Ethelbert Stauffer, *New Testament Theology*, trans. J. Marsh (New York: Macmillan, 1955), pp. 331–334.

5. H. B. Swete, *The Apocalypse of St. John* (London: Macmillan, 1906), p. 165.

6. Text widely available; here from J. Stevenson (ed.), *A New Eusebius* (New York: Seabury, 1957), p. 13.

7. Robert M. Grant, *The Apostolic Fathers: Volume I, An Introduction* (New York: Thomas Nelson, 1964), p. 90. Quoted with permission.

8. Edgar J. Goodspeed, *The Apostolic Fathers: An American Translation* (New York: Harper & Row, 1950), pp. 250f.; from "The Martyrdom of Polycarp."

9. *Ibid.*, p. 278, from "The Address to Diognetus."

10. Tertullian, *Apology*, iv. 3–5; from *The Fathers of the Church* edition.

11. Origen, *Contra Celsum*, V, 37; from the translation by H. Chadwick.

12. S. L. Greenslade (ed.), *Early Latin Theology*, in "The Library of Christian Classics" (Philadelphia: Westminster Press, 1956), p. 215.

13. Hans van Campenhausen, *Men Who Shaped the Western Church* (New York: Harper & Row, 1965), p. 112.

14. S. L. Greenslade, *The Church and the Social Order* (London: S.C.M., 1948), p. 30. Quoted with permission.

15. In Greenslade (ed.), *Early Latin Theology*, p. 214.

16. R. H. C. Davis, *A History of Medieval Europe* (London: Longmans, 1963), p. 247.

17. Bk. IV, ch. vii; Dickinson ed., p. 33.

18. E. R. Fairweather (ed.), *A Scholastic Miscellany: Anselm to Ockham*, in "The Library of Christian Classics" (Philadelphia: Westminster Press, 1956), p. 258.

19. C. C. J. Webb, *John of Salisbury*, in "Great Medieval Churchmen" series (London: Methuen, 1932), gives a sympathetic account of the life, character, and thought of its subject. The remarks on tyrannicide are on pp. 65ff.

20. *S.T.*, Ia, IIae, qu. 96. 4.

21. *Ibid.*

22. *S.T.*, IIa, IIae, qu. 104. 6.

23. George H. Sabine, *A History of Political Theory* (New York: Henry Holt, 1949), p. 311.

24. J. N. Figgis, *The Divine Right of Kings* (2nd ed., Cam-

bridge University Press, 1922), p. 70. The author cites here Wycliffe's *De officio regis.*

4. THE TRADITION OF CHRISTIAN DISSENT (2)

1. Martin Luther, "Treatise on Good Works," in J. Atkinson
(ed.), *Luther's Works,* Vol. 44, *The Christian in Society,* I (Philadelphia: Fortress Press, 1966), p. 92.

2. *Ibid.,* p. 93.

3. *Ibid.,* p. 81.

4. See Lowell C. Green, "Resistance to Authority and Luther,"
in *The Lutheran Quarterly,* Vol. VI, No. 4 (November, 1954), pp.
338ff. See also Cyril Richardson, "Prophecy and Politics: A Study
in Martin Luther," in *Review of Religion,* Vol. I (January, 1947),
pp. 136ff. Richardson identifies four stages in the development of
Luther's political stance.

5. Luther, *op. cit.,* p. 100.

6. The authority of the Augsburg Confession, for example, can
be cited in favor of disobedience. Article XVI says in part: "Christians are obliged to be subject to civil authority and obey its commands and laws in all that can be done without sin. But when
commands of the civil authority cannot be obeyed without sin, we
must obey God rather than men" (Acts 5:29).

Some of the best writing on the state and on civil disobedience
emerging in modern times from the Lutheran tradition is in Eivind
Berggrav, *Man and State,* trans. G. Aus (Philadelphia: Muhlen-
berg, 1951). Bishop Berggrav cites Luther in criticism of the state
very effectively. In the Lutheran tradition see also the closing paragraphs of the statement on race relations adopted by the Lutheran
Church in America in July, 1964, quoted in Appendix II of this
book.

7. Calvin, *Institutes,* IV, xx, 4.

8. Robert Meyners, "An Investigation of the Basis for Christian
Resistance to Civil Authority" (an unpublished doctoral thesis at
Union Theological Seminary, New York, 1958), p. 23.

9. Calvin, *Institutes,* IV, xx, 31.

10. Meyners, unpublished doctoral thesis, *op. cit.,* p. 24.

11. Sabine, *A History of Political Thought* (New York: Henry Holt, 1949), p. 377. An edition of the *Vindiciae* was published in 1924 as *A Defense of Liberty against Tyrants* (New York: Harcourt, Brace). It contains a fine historical and expository introduction by H. J. Laski.

12. J. N. Figgis, *Studies of Political Thought from Gerson to Grotius 1414–1625* (2nd ed.; Cambridge: Cambridge University Press, 1931), Chap. II, pp. 31–54. See also Sabine, *op. cit.*, pp. 385–391.

13. Quoted in Figgis, *The Divine Right of Kings* (2nd ed.; Cambridge: Cambridge University Press, 1922), p. 385. The passage is from Nelson, *Common Interest of King and People.*

14. The First Part of "An Homily against Disobedience and Wilful Rebellion."

15. *E.P.*, VIII, ii, 10, is a passage in which Hooker seems to approach the subject. But the passage is far from clear or decisive in declaring a specific view.

16. *E.P.*, I, x, 8; cf. also VIII, vi, 8 and 11.

17. *E.P.*, VIII, viii, 9.

18. From the Constitutions and Canons Ecclesiastical of 1640, Canon I, "Concerning the Regal Power." The text is in Cardwell's *Synodalia*, I, pp. 389ff.

19. III, Chap. 1, Rule 1. This paragraph follows Taylor's succeeding rules.

20. Thomas Wood, *English Casuistical Divinity during the Seventeenth Century* (London: S.P.C.K., 1952), p. 85, summarizing Taylor.

21. *Ibid.*, p. 86.

22. A. Peel and L. H. Carlson (eds.), *The Writings of Robert Harrison and Robert Browne* (London: Allen and Unwin, 1953), pp. 158f.

23. John Bunyan, *Grace Abounding and The Pilgrim's Progress,* ed. John Brown (Cambridge: Cambridge University Press, 1907), pp. 125f.

24. Text from Joseph A. Blau (ed.), *Cornerstones of Religious Freedom in America* (New York: Harper Torchbooks, 1964), pp. 36f.

25. *Ibid.*, p. 69.

26. Edmund S. Morgan, "The American Revolution Considered as an Intellectual Movement," in A. Schlesinger and M. White (eds.), *Paths of American Thought* (Boston: Houghton Mifflin, 1963), pp. 13f.

27. Clinton Rossiter, *The Political Thought of the American Revolution* (New York: Harcourt, Brace & World, 1963), p. 8.

28. Cambridge: Harvard University Press, 1966.

29. Portions of this sermon are often anthologized. The entire (quite lengthy) text is in the interesting old book: John W. Thornton, *The Pulpit of the American Revolution* (Boston: Gould and Lincoln, 1860); the passage quoted is on pp. 87f. A fine interpretive biography of Mayhew is Charles W. Akers, *Called Unto Liberty* (Cambridge: Harvard University Press, 1964).

30. Cited in Bernard Bailyn, *The Ideological Origins of the American Revolution* (Cambridge: Harvard University Press, 1967), p. 93.

31. Edward H. Madden, *Civil Disobedience and Moral Law in Nineteenth-Century American Philosophy* (Seattle: University of Washington, 1968), p. 37.

32. Text from L. Schlissel (ed.), *Conscience in America* (New York: Dutton, 1968), pp. 83ff.

33. From Louis Filler (ed.), *Wendell Phillips on Civil Rights and Freedom* (New York: Hill & Wang, 1965), pp. 107f.

34. Madden, *op. cit.,* pp. 80f. Quoted with permission.

5. THE OBEDIENCE WHICH MUST DISOBEY

1. First of the "evangelical truths" in the Barmen Declaration. A. C. Cochrane, *The Church's Confession under Hitler* (Philadelphia: Westminster Press, 1962), p. 239.

2. Deuteronomy 6:4. The text is, of course, the Jewish Shema, which is repeated frequently in synagogue worship rather as a confession of faith.

3. For Jesus and the Father, cf. Matthew 11:27 and context; John 3:35; 4:34; 5:20; 13:3; and the Fourth Gospel *passim*; Luke 23:46. On the primacy of the kingdom, Matthew 13:44–46.

4. Cf. Isaiah 17:13f.; 40:12–31; Jeremiah 10:10; 50:44–46; Amos 1 and 2; 5:18–20; Mark 13:32–37.

5. Dietrich Bonhoeffer, *Letters and Papers from Prison,* ed. Bethge; trans. Fuller (London: SCM, 1953), p. 179, speaks of "man existing for others, and hence the Crucified." J. A. T. Robinson, *Honest to God* (London: SCM, 1963), adapts the phrase on p. 76 and uses it, in his adapted form, as the title for chapter 4.

6. H. Richard Niebuhr, *Radical Monotheism and Western Culture* (New York: Harper & Row, 1960), p. 34.

7. John Oman, *Grace and Personality* (2nd ed.; Cambridge: Cambridge University Press, 1919), p. 167.

8. Cited in Stephen Neill, *Man in God's Purpose* (New York: Association Press, n.d.), p. 27. Bishop Neill gives no source for his quotation, and a search of several of Temple's works has not located it. But it summarizes concisely a view of sin which Temple expounded frequently in similar terms.

9. Helmut Gollwitzer, *The Demands of Freedom* (New York: Harper & Row, 1965), pp. 67f.

10. John C. Bennett, *Christians and the State* (New York: Scribners, 1958), p. 75.

11. Carl L. Becker, *Freedom and Responsibility in the American Way of Life* (New York: Vintage Books, 1955), p. 98.

12. Harold Laski, *Introduction to Politics* (New York: Barnes & Noble, 1963), pp. 15f. Quoted with permission.

13. Cf. *ibid.,* p. 18: "But if I ask why I should be expected to obey the state, it is clearly not sufficient to tell me that I must obey it because it is the state. I shall ask, as men in the past have asked, why the dictates of the state deserve obedience; and if those dictates contradict all that I think and hope and feel, I may well conclude, as men in the past have concluded, that I have no alternative open to me but to refuse the obedience thus demanded of me."

14. Edmond Cahn, *The Predicament of Democratic Man* (New York: Macmillan, 1961), pp. 77ff. The seven pages on which these questions are set forth with Cahn's explanations of their import is a passage of very great merit.

15. Quoted in *ibid.,* p. 101.

16. Dietrich Bonhoeffer, *Ethics* (New York: Macmillan, 1965), p. 181. Quoted with permission.

6. THE CONDITIONS OF RESPONSIBLE DISOBEDIENCE

1. Meyners, unpublished doctoral thesis, *op. cit.*, p. 393.

2. Quoted by Robert Drinan, S.J., in "Lawyers and Nonviolent Demonstrations," an address reprinted in *The Catholic Worker,* June, 1964. Father Drinan does not give his source in Thoreau.

3. Colossians 1:17. Professor Moule's commentary paraphrases: "The universe owes its coherence to him."

4. Reinhold Niebuhr, "God's Design and the Present Disorder of Civilization," in *Man's Disorder and God's Design* (New York: Harper & Row, n.d.), Part II, pp. 26f. Quoted with permission.

5. Drinan, *op. cit.;* cf. Frankel, *The Love of Anxiety* (New York: Harper & Row, 1965), p. 176: "There is the simple but painful factor of time. If a man is holding you down on a bed of nails, it is all very well for a bystander to say that you live in a great country in which there are legal remedies for your condition, and that you ought, therefore, to be patient and wait for those remedies to take effect. But your willingness to listen to this counsel will depend, quite properly, on the nature of the injury you are suffering."

6. Drinan, *op. cit.*

7. Gollwitzer, *The Demands of Freedom* (New York: Harper & Row, 1965), p. 70.

8. Carl Cohen, "Essence and Ethics of Civil Disobedience," in *The Nation,* March 16, 1964, p. 258.

9. Drinan, *op. cit.*

10. Frankel, *op. cit.*, p. 179.

11. William Temple, *Christian Faith and Life* (New York: Macmillan, 1931), pp. 61f.

12. Meyners, unpublished doctoral thesis, *op. cit.*, p. 396.

13. Increasingly, at least for the present, the Negro does not feel that he needs or wants the white; those whites who wish to identify with the black cause will have to find ways of working which accept the depth and reality of this rejection—indeed, which welcome the stage of development it signals. Bayard Rustin spoke of progress gained by Negroes and commented: "And not one

white person was needed. Is it good to have them? Spiritually it is a profound thing to have them, but they were not needed. I am talking about social reality." "Nonviolence on Trial," in Staughton Lynd (ed.), *Nonviolence in America: A Documentary History* (New York: Bobbs Merrill, 1966), p. 489. These paragraphs of this chapter are a possible commentary on Rustin's words, "Spiritually it is a profound thing to have them."

14. Frankel, *op. cit.*, p. 180.

15. Edward LeRoy Long, Jr., *War and Conscience in America* (Philadelphia: Westminster Press, 1968), pp. 97f.

7. AN EXAMINATION OF CHRISTIAN NONVIOLENCE

1. Quoted in W. R. Miller, *Nonviolence: A Christian Interpretation* (New York: Association Press, 1964), p. 303.

2. The text is Matthew 5:39 from the Sermon on the Mount. The object in the sentence can, in Greek, be either neuter, "evil" (which sounds like a universal ethical maxim) or masculine, "him that is evil" (which makes it refer more to wrong inflicted by a personal enemy).

3. Tolstoy's most accessible statements are *The Kingdom of God Is within You,* reissued in paperback (New York: Noonday Press, 1961), and *Tolstoy's Writings on Civil Disobedience and Nonviolence* (New York: Signet Books, 1968).

4. Gandhi's ideas and their relation to Hindu and Christian sources are briefly treated in Miller, *op. cit.,* pp. 24–31. A fuller discussion is in Stephen Neill, *Christian Faith and Other Faiths* (London: Oxford University Press, 1961), pp. 77ff. In addition to being a reader of the Gospels and an admirer of Jesus, Gandhi drew Western influence from Thoreau. This debt is traced in George Hendrick, "The Influence of Thoreau's 'Civil Disobedience' on Gandhi's *Satyagraha,*" reprinted in Owen Thomas (ed.), *Walden and Civil Disobedience* (New York: W. W. Norton, 1966).

5. Miller, *op. cit.,* pp. 24–29.

6. See Neill, *op. cit.,* p. 78.

7. Dietrich Bonhoeffer, *The Cost of Discipleship* (New York: Macmillan, 1956), p. 125.

8. *Ibid.*

9. A point made in J. Thayer Addison, *War, Peace and the Christian Mind* (New York: Seabury Press, 1953), p. 38. Addison cites here John Lewis, *The Case against Pacifism*.

10. Hannah Arendt, *On Revolution* (New York: Viking Press, 1967), pp. 10f. Quoted with permission.

11. Kenneth B. Clark, *Dark Ghetto* (New York: Harper & Row, 1965), p. 206.

12. Addison, *op. cit.,* pp. 66f., citing here G. C. Field, *Pacifism and Conscientious Objection*.

13. Miller, *op. cit.,* pp. 156ff.

14. This phase of the development of Bonhoeffer's thought and sense of calling is described in John D. Godsey, *The Theology of Dietrich Bonhoeffer* (London: SCM, 1960), pp. 195–203.

8. Revolution and Obedience

1. A piece of intelligence for which I am indebted to D. W. Brogan, *American Aspects* (New York: Harper & Row, 1964), p. 22.

2. It is difficult to know for how long a time the term should be made applicable. The "era of revolution" is usually spoken of in recent literature as a development of just the last few years. But in Sir Denis Brogan's *The Price of Revolution,* written in 1951, the fact that we are living in an age of revolution is cited as a matter of common consent. In 1952 the late Archbishop Garbett wrote a wise book, *In an Age of Revolution*. It was retrospective in character summarizing the meaning of changes that had taken place in the society and the church within his memory. It is possible, of course, to push the awareness of fairly continuous revolution back still further. 1848 or 1775 are likely candidates for the start of such an age. Brogan seems to vote for the earlier of these dates. A. R. Vidler's recent history of the church since 1789 is called *The Church and the Age of Revolution*. It is not necessary to set a time for the start of our present "age of revolution," and it would certainly be unwise to look back historically so hard that qualitative differences in contemporary consciousness were overlooked in the effort to demonstrate that it had all happened before. But it

is worth noting that the awareness of living in revolutionary times has been with us for a great while.

3. Hannah Arendt, *On Revolution*, p. 219.

4. The text of this passage from "The Declaration of Independence" is from Richard Hofstadter (ed.), *Great Issues in American History: A Documentary Record* (New York: Vintage Books, 1958), Vol. 1, p. 71.

5. Emil Brunner, *The Divine Imperative*, trans. Olive Wyon (Philadelphia: Westminster Press, 1947), pp. 218, 618. Copyright 1947 by W. L. Jenkins. Quoted with permission.

6. Harvey Cox, *The Secular City* (New York: Macmillan, 1965), p. 107.

7. Luke 1:51–53, echoing I Samuel 2:6–8; Job 5:11; Psalm 75:6, 7; Psalm 147:6; Ezekiel 21:26; Ecclesiasticus 10:14; I Corinthians 1:26–28.

8. Thoreau, "Civil Disobedience."

9. Brogan, *The Price of Revolution* (New York: Grosset & Dunlap, 1966 ed.), p. 11. This book by Professor Brogan is probably the best cautionary tale available on the subject of revolution.

Select Bibliography

: :

The following list of books and articles is quite selective. The quantity of material specifically on civil disobedience itself is not great. In the supporting categories, the potential material is very extensive.

ON CIVIL DISOBEDIENCE

Fortas, Abe, *Concerning Dissent and Civil Disobedience*. New York: Signet Books, 1968. A slight, but more than competent, "broadside" on the subject. Justice Fortas seems not always to be fully aware of the depth of the issues seen by dissenters. But the booklet is valuable for the personal, humane spirit in which it is written. The author is particularly concerned that the established legal structures be flexible and responsive to felt needs so that the society has "an alternative to violence."

Frankel, Charles, "The Morality of Civil Disobedience," in *The Love of Anxiety*. New York: Harper & Row, 1965. This essay (published originally in *The New York Times Magazine*) is one of the finest brief statements available.

Meyners, Robert, *An Investigation of the Basis for Christian Resistance to Civil Authority*. An unpublished dissertation presented to the faculty of the Union Theological Seminary, New York, in 1958. This is a very thorough study of certain aspects of the subject. It is a mine of insights and information. It is based on close investigation of certain European theologians. The analysis of the attitudes toward disobedience of these representative thinkers is very acute. The book, however, is an academic exercise and suffers from the necessity of conforming to thesis requirements. The author had too little freedom to develop the constructive, independent ideas which press to the surface—especially in the later sections. Even though this work was done only ten years ago, so much has happened in those intervening years that it seems not to speak to the contemporary situation with the clarity a present-day reader might wish for. Yet it gains by its closeness to the experience of passive obedience and courageous disobedience on the part of Christians under Hitler. Its general historical material is sketchy. It is narrow in its focus and flawed as a comprehensive treatment. Yet it is a spendid work, and—as a theological study—almost the only thorough piece of research in the field. It might be termed the finest work now unavailable on the subject.

Thoreau, Henry, *Civil Disobedience.* This classic essay is available in many editions including several in paperback.

────── "On Civil Disobedience, 1967," in *The New York Times Magazine,* November 26, 1967. Thirteen short statements on civil disobedience by eminent, articulate persons representing a wide variety of opinions.

New Testament and Early Christian Material

Cullmann, Oscar, *The State in the New Testament.* New York: Scribners, 1956.

Frend, W. H. C., *Martyrdom and Persecution in the Early Church.* New York: Doubleday, 1967. Scholarly, informative, and unfailingly interesting. It includes pre-Christian Jewish history.

Morrison, Clinton D., *The Powers That Be.* London: S. C. M. Press, 1960.

Reumann, John, and Lazareth, William, *Righteousness and Society.* Philadelphia: Fortress Press, 1967. The first half of this book, by Professor Reumann, is a very valuable account of the social posture of the early church.

Wilder, Amos N., *Kerygma, Eschatology, and Social Ethics.* Philadelphia: Fortress Press, 1967. A brief but valuable study.

HISTORICAL MATERIAL

There is no history of Christian civil disobedience. Most of the material for the subject is traceable in standard sources. For recent periods (especially American), several books are available which give extracts from essential sources not otherwise easily found. These books tend to be organized around pacifism rather than civil disobedience, but the two subjects meet at many points.

Lynd, Staughton (ed.), *Nonviolence in America: A Documentary History*. New York: Bobbs Merrill, 1966. Well-chosen material, well introduced.

Madden, Edward H., *Civil Disobedience and Moral Law in Nineteenth-Century American Philosophy*. Seattle: University of Washington, 1968. Recent, scholarly, interesting.

Mayer, Peter (ed.), *The Pacifist Conscience*. New York: Holt, Rinehart, & Winston, 1966. Another gathering of documents; valuable for its inclusion of ancient and non-Western sources.

Schlissel, Lillian (ed.), *Conscience in America: A Documentary History of Conscientious Objection in America, 1757–1967*. New York: Dutton, 1968. The title identifies conscience with only one course of conduct; aside from this presumption, a good collection.

Tolstoy, Leo, *Tolstoy's Writings on Civil Disobedience and Nonviolence*. New York: Signet Books, 1968. A fascinating collection.

ON NONVIOLENCE

King, Martin Luther, "Pilgrimage to Nonviolence," in *Stride Toward Freedom*. New York: Harper & Row, 1958. King's own account of his intellectual development and the people, ideas, and events that influenced him.

Miller, William Robert, *Nonviolence: A Christian Interpretation*. New York: Association Press, 1964; paperback edition published by Schocken Books, New York. An excellent, comprehensive study.

Regamey, Pie, O.P., *Non-Violence and the Christian Conscience*. New York: Herder & Herder, 1966. A penetrating ethical study by a French Roman Catholic.

REVOLUTION

Arendt, Hannah, *On Revolution*. New York: Viking Press, 1965.
  Miss Arendt seems somewhat bemused by the idea that
  revolution must be proletarian; but this is a book with great
  insight and intellectual power.

Bennett, John C. (ed.), *Christian Social Ethics in a Changing
  World*. New York: Association Press, 1966. An ecumenical
  survey with articles at a generally very high level.

Berdyaev, Nikolai, *Slavery and Freedom*. New York: Scribners,
  1944. Put on this list for its many excellences but particularly
  for some extremely provocative pages in Part III. 2.A. The
  contemporary writers on revolution are only catching up with
  Berdyaev.

Matthews, Z. K. (ed.), *Responsible Government in a Revolutionary
  Age*. New York: Association Press, 1966. An ecumenical
  symposium—a companion to the volume above edited by
  Bennett.

Oglesby, Carl, and Shaull, Richard, *Containment and Change*.
  New York: Macmillan, 1967. Shaull is one of the most
  articulate of the writers on a theology of revolution; his highly
  characteristic contribution to this book will introduce the main
  themes of his thought. His numerous articles should also be
  noted.

INDEX

Ambrose, 49f., 52

American society; alienated groups in, 11f., 15f.; created by revolution, 67; divided, 119; intentions corrupted, 15, 21; legalism of, 67, 105f.

Antigone (Sophocles), 39f., 191

Apocrypha, I and II Maccabees, 43; Wisdom of Solomon 6: 1–5, 24, 34

Aquinas, Thomas, 8, 53f.

Arendt, Hannah, 130, 141

Augsburg Confession, 193

Augustine, 8, 50f.

Barmen Declaration, 80

Becker, Carl, 90

Bennett, John C., 18, 22, 26, 89

Bible, authority of, 22f.; "inverting motif," 143f.

Bonhoeffer, Dietrich, 83 and n.5, 99, 127, 137f.

Bornkamm, G., 34

Borowitz, Eugene B., 190

Brogan, D. W., 139 n.1, 156 and n.9

Brown, John, 73f., 162

Browne, Robert, 65f.

Brunner, Emil, 142f.

Bunyan, John, 66

Cahn, Edmond, 94

Calvin, John, 8, 58f.

Campenhausen, H. von, 49 n.13

Church, called to service of man, 83f.; community in Christ, 80; community of discussion, 101f.; community of identification, 120; dependent on Christ, 66, 80; divided, 81, 119; a force for reconciliation, 84; may have to oppose the state, 85; must relate duty to the gospel, 80; recognizes absolute claim of God, 81f.; seeks the mind of Christ, 118f.; sinful, 86

Church statements on civil disobedience, adequacy and authority of statements, viii; Lutheran Church in America, 172f.; National Council of Churches 166ff.; Presbyterian Church in the United States, 173f.; Protestant Episcopal Church, 174; Roman Catholic Church, 164f.; United Methodist Church, 175; United Presbyterian Church in the USA, 175f.; World Conference on Church and Society, 165f.